Wedding Etiquette

HELL

Wedding Etiquette

HELL

The Bride's Bible to Avoiding Everlasting Damnation

Jeanne Hamilton

Thomas Dunne Books
St. Martin's Griffin ⚭ New York

THOMAS DUNNE BOOKS.
An imprint of St. Martin's Press.

www.stmartins.com

Etiquette Hell is a registered trademark.

Library of Congress Cataloging-in-Publication Data

Hamilton, Jeanne.
    Wedding etiquette hell : the bride's bible to avoiding everlasting
damnation / Jeanne Hamilton.
        p. cm.
    ISBN 0-312-33023-5
    EAN 978-0312-33023-1
    1. Wedding etiquette.   2. Weddings—Planning.   I. Title.
BJ2051.H36 2005
395.2'2—dc22   2004065660

First Edition: June 2005

10 9 8 7 6 5 4 3 2 1

To Tim

Contents

Acknowledgments

I would like to thank my dear husband, who has been my staunchest supporter, my best editor, my rock of standards, and one of the most gentlemanly persons of my acquaintance. Thank you for stopping whatever work you were doing to listen to hundreds of Etiquette-Hell.com stories. A hearty thank-you to my three children, who shouldered the housecleaning, cooking, and yardwork while I was working on the book. Thank you to Phil, who continues to appreciate the irony. My gratitude also goes to my agent, Stephanie Rostan, who has been the model of gracious professionalism and friendship. I would also like to thank St. Martin's Press, for believing in the Etiquette Hell concept and helping save brides everywhere from damnation. And finally, thank you to the fans who make EtiquetteHell.com the interesting and rewarding place that it is.

Introduction

Few know what they're doing. They are endowed with incredible authority, are pressured to please everyone, and produce the effects of a dictatorship within the strictures of democracy. —ELISE MAC ADAM

GLAD TIDINGS! YOU ARE ENGAGED to be married! You may be reading this book because you are, as brides across the Western world are, genetically hardwired to hightail it to the bookstore to rummage through stacks of three-ring-binder wedding planners and four-inch-thick tomes known as etiquette books as soon as Romeo rises from his kneeling proposal. Most brides become etiquette scholars for the duration of their wedding planning, studying these textbooks of anti-tackiness with the seriousness of a Ph.D. candidate.

But what passes for "etiquette" is often nothing more than glorified traditions with entire chapters devoted to diamond cuts, carat weights, what certain flowers signify, the color of the wedding dress, fifty zillion ways to address an envelope, lists of music choices, and how a groom can remove the bride's garter with his teeth with the utmost decorum. Even worse, there is the "new etiquette," often touted on Internet wedding Web sites, which throws real etiquette away entirely and gives brides carte blanche to do whatever their little bridal hearts desire.

From the time the engagement ring encircles the finger to the start of the honeymoon, a bride and groom walk a tightrope across a wedding-planning chasm. They are constantly trying to balance their desires for the perfect wedding with the expectations of guests and family, aiming for the target of a wedding everyone enjoys. The wedding-planning path is fraught with opportunities to dive right into Etiquette Hell. You have the opportunity to do this well, to the blessing of all, or do this poorly, to the detriment of those whom you love.

Your wedding is hugely important to you; it can also have a huge effect upon those around you and your relationships with them. Friends and family can be silent victims of bridal wrath if things go wrong or of bridal indifference if things go right. They bear their wounds without comment, lest they be accused of "ruining" the wedding day. Many brides skip merrily along, totally unaware of how bad their behavior is, while their friends and family pour out their grievances to me, Miss Jeanne, at www.etiquettehell.com. What they may have been afraid to tell the bride, they tell me in graphic detail.

Many faux pas occur from simple ignorance, raising the possibility of "tripping" accidentally into Etiquette Hell. However, victims of your accidental faux pas won't always be forgiving, nor will they be tolerant of your ignorance or aware of your good intentions. All they know is that you stepped all over their toes and it hurts! Emily Post is too polite to tell you the consequences of eschewing her etiquette advice. I have no such inhibitions in sounding the warning alarm that something is a bit amiss and heading south fast.

People do not nominate their nuptially minded friends and family for inclusion in Etiquette Hell for little slights that should be overlooked as part of loving one another. (And if they do, I boot them into Etiquette Hell themselves for pettiness.) Who really cares whether you wear a gold dress instead of white, or whether you have suits or tuxes on the groomsmen, or whether the reception punch matches the color of the bridesmaids' dresses? Inconsequential decisions that are often defined as "etiquette" are not issues people care enough about to damn a couple into eternal social ostracism forever and ever, amen. The ire rises to the boiling point only when people are abused with presumptions on their time, finances, and generosity. Then they start banging out on their keyboard a flurry of verbiage venting their frustration to the concerned eyes of Miss Jeanne.

So, how does a bride execute the biggest social extravaganza of her life without ending up a social pariah? Unless the bride can afford the luxury of a wedding planner who handles every detail from *A* to *Z*, she faces the daunting task of coordinating a complicated event while meeting all the expectations of family, friends, vendors, and guests. Existing peacefully in society requires a delicate balance among all individuals, a certain amount of reciprocal courtesy and kindness. The stories presented in this book illustrate numerous civility rules. They are from real people about real brides and grooms. They are representative of the thousands of e-mails I receive annually bemoaning the loss of civility in our culture. While Miss Manners or Emily Post may wag their fingers and say, No, no, thou shalt not!, my presenting firsthand accounts of offended guests and friends has a greater "grassroots" impact that causes brides to sit up and pay attention.

Wedding Etiquette Hell dismisses the stuffy fluff of high-society etiquette rules and concerns itself with issues of etiquette that really matter to people: what offends them, what inspires them to snickers of derision, what compels them to quietly put you on their "no more gifts in my lifetime" list or drop you off their social radar.

The focus of this book is the way you should behave as you attempt to coordinate the largest event of your life. In effect, you are the CEO of a limited-engagement endeavor, and your leadership will affect the motivation and morale of your "staff." Human nature being what it is, even your best friends and closest family are still fallible beings and will make occasional gaffes or even present outright opposition to your well-thought-out plans. The way you handle these interpersonal relationships during the stressful parts of wedding planning will depend on your talent for diplomacy. It may also require your willingness to do the right thing despite the temptation to let fly with some deliciously rude remark to some nincompoop desperately deserving of your disdain.

Being civil does not mean you are a doormat, giving up all your hopes, dreams, and plans in order to keep the peace among friends and family. However, if you are asking people to expend time and money for your wedding, there has to be some consideration of their input and some effort at moving toward an equitable compromise that leaves everyone content. "But it's my day!" you exclaim with some indignation. Isn't this the day you've been waiting for your whole life? Isn't it your "turn" to get the attention and have the party of your dreams? If the front covers of many wedding magazines are an indication, the wedding allegedly consists of only the bride; it is entirely "her day." However, ponder for a moment just what a wedding is and who is involved. A wedding is a celebration and confirmation of relationships—the joining of two people, of two families, and of two sets of friends. You'll be happier and your attendants will be, too, if you approach wedding planning with a balanced perspective that includes a concern for the well-being of the people and the relationships involved, rather than concentrating only on how to execute the perfect wedding production!

Throughout the chapters of this book, there is an ongoing wedding-planning dialogue with our fictional bride, Brideweena, and her wedding coordinator, Miss Jeanne.

Our Cast of Characters includes:

Miss Jeanne: Our venerable wedding coordinator. She's been there, done that, and isn't afraid to lay down the law. She'll tell her clients with clarity just what the consequences of their choices may be, and sometimes it isn't pretty.

Brideweena: Our lovely bride. She thinks she knows what she wants only because that's how everyone else did it. Her etiquette sense is cobbled together from reading too many wedding magazines and Web sites, and listening to her well-meaning but sometimes mistaken friends.

Curtis: Brideweena's fiancé. He's interested primarily in what the menu is for the reception and has little involvement in the wedding planning. It would be nice if he were more involved, but he sees all this wedding planning as the domain of the women.

Ethell: Brideweena's mom. She thinks she knows what she wants and is not shy in telling Brideweena what to do.

Uncle Frito, Aunt Fifi, and **Little Darling Fufu:** The relatives. You know, those relatives . . .

Muffin Louise: Brideweena's best friend and matron of honor. Her wedding was several months earlier and it wasn't a pretty sight. Carnage and relational devastation everywhere.

This book cannot possibly cover every conceivable scenario that can occur with a wedding. If it did, the book would be ten inches thick. It does, however, cover the most common and inconsiderate mistakes brides sometimes make. It portrays real-life wedding train wrecks and gives you the tools and insights to avoid them. Its wisdom is not difficult or stuffy or obscure. If you keep three important principles in mind—the importance of respect, a willingness to compromise, and an unwillingness to presume upon people—you should be well on your way to the perfect wedding day!

ONE

The Devil Is in the Details

Weddings are fabulous crucibles that reveal the true
characters of those involved. —ELIZABETH YORK

JUST AS SOON AS THAT RING is firmly ensconced on the left
hand, a magical transformation occurs. It may effect a delight-
ful change in the bearer, who adopts a sincere and enlightened
altruism and noble gentility about the wedding-planning journey she
is undertaking together with her beloved groom, family, and friends.
Or the ringbearer can disappear altogether, with the creature that
emerges having no resemblance to the bride's former self. The ring has
become a burdensome "Precious" that transforms its wearer into a
despicable, self-serving wretch. The latter type of bride proceeds
down the aisle under the enchanted misperception that she is the most
beautiful of women when she is in reality a pitiable creature feared by
some and despised by most.

How well you cross the wedding-planning chasm will be deter-
mined largely by the attitudes you bring to the process and whether
you choose to succumb to the dark side of the Wedding Force. The
sweetly whispered temptations are many and the opportunities to fail
frequent, but I'll help you navigate through the morass and come out

the other side as a radiant bride who has inspired gratitude and fond memories in her loved ones.

Rule 1: Money and Rock Size Are Taboo Subjects

Sheri got engaged before me and went on and on about her gorgeous ring, how she never took it off (even to bathe), how it came from some exotic country, was the only one cut like that, how much it cost, etc. Her ring was amazingly huge and I complimented it several times, even after she began sharing all the inappropriate details about it. She also gave me all the details on her custom-made $10,000 dress and how much the bridesmaids' dresses were costing (last count was $500). Cut to a few months later, when I got engaged. Sheri sent an e-mail to congratulate me, but the only comment in the e-mail was, "What cut and clarity is the diamond, and how many carats?" Her words exactly. I didn't bother replying to that.

It's crass and uncouth to discuss money. How much a person earns and how much something costs are taboo questions to ask other people. Tacky, very tacky. It is equally tacky to brag about how much money was spent on elements of the wedding. (Want to know a secret? We couldn't care less if your dress is a Poochi Diva Original costing fifteen thousand dollars for that unadorned sliver of fabric.)

Brides who obsess over diamond size and cost give the feminine gender a bad name by drooling over a choice diamond like bone-hungry dogs. It gives the impression that all you care about is wealth accumulation. If the glittering boulder adorning your heavily bejeweled left hand isn't obvious enough, your friends and family really don't need you flaunting the price tag, too.

Immutable Fact of Life

Be so crass as to brag about how much you spent on flowers, dress, or photographer, and your guests will start speculating how much you spent to entertain them. A perception of a negative balance will not endear you to them, so keep your mouth shut.

Rule 2: Moderation in Everything, Including Moderation

I have too many stories to tell but this one takes the cake. This is a story of tackiness and greed. After a friend of mine got engaged they had an engagement party. That was fine, I bought a gift and went. A couple months later they had another engagement party held by his parents (yes, another engagement gift was expected). The next month another. A total of three engagement parties. Next came the bridal showers. I was invited to three of her bridal showers. I was a friend of the groom so did not feel the need to be at each shower, however I did go to the first with a gift. Next comes the prewedding party. I have never heard of a prewedding party. Then the wedding and last but not least a gift-opening party (they sent out invitations to this event as well, with a note of another place they had a registry). And yes, they did expect you to bring another gift. Had I showed up to all of their parties with gifts, I would have bought eight or nine gifts. This was just plain crazy to me but some people did not mind or were too embarrassed to say anything or to not bring a gift. They got all that they wanted from all four places they registered.

Is it really necessary to have three engagement parties? Traditionally, engagement parties were hosted by the parents with the announcement of the engagement kept secret from the guests to squelch any notion that the party was a gift-giving opportunity. As can be seen, some guests interpret these invitations as requiring them to come bearing gifts even if there are not registry cards or information plastered everywhere. (Note to all future wedding guests: one shower gift and one wedding gift is generosity aplenty for any wedding.)

There should be some moderation in the total number of parties, showers, and gift openings guests are invited to attend. Whether you like it or not, people do interpret an overabundance of gift-centered parties as being greedy. So the engagement should not be viewed as a scheduled series of events all designed to maximize the likelihood of acquiring registered gifts.

Rule 3: No Dueling Wedding Dates

When I first met my friend Audrey, the first thing she did was tell me that her "baby sister" was engaged and that the wedding was to be a year and a half later. I didn't think much of this information, just something that a new acquaintance—later, friend—was sharing about her life. I quickly realized that Audrey, at thirty-nine, was desperate to get married and have babies. She soon met Roger, and within five months of meeting, they became engaged.

After that, I was constantly barraged by Audrey e-mailing me photos of wedding dresses, telling me her plans, and almost every wedding-related conversation ended with her wailing, "What's a bride to do?" I kept reminding myself to be patient, that in her place, I'd probably drive my friends just as crazy without realizing it. In addition, the entire time, Audrey made it clear that she didn't like her sister's wedding plans, didn't like her sister's bachelorette party plans, and didn't like her sister's choice of groom. I was invited to a party that their family was giving, and since her sister's wedding was to be in two months, that was naturally the topic of conversation. It soon became obvious that what Audrey didn't like was her younger sister getting all the attention.

Then the kicker came. It was almost time for Audrey's sister's wedding. Audrey and Roger, being pagan, decided to plan a handfast-ing ceremony for themselves that was to take place two weeks before her sister's wedding. For those unfamiliar with handfastings, it is usually a "promise" to marry, as opposed to a marriage ceremony itself. (It can be ei-ther, I would like to note.) However, I was given the dis-tinct impression that this would be the "promise" ceremony, not the "marriage" ceremony.

So the guests arrive to the handfasting—and to my surprise, it was the actual marriage ceremony. Audrey's sister had come—but she looked extremely upset. I can't say I blame her. I found myself suspecting the worst—that Audrey had pushed up her wedding to beat her sister. I told my-self that I was being silly, that since Audrey had been planning the big fussy wedding, there was surely a good reason that she suddenly went for something small and simple.

However, my worst suspicions were confirmed when Audrey came back from her sister's wedding. I asked how it was, and instead of the usual, "It was lovely, thanks for asking," I got a very smug, "It was better than I'd hoped, since now I wasn't the spinster older sister!" I think the saddest thing about this is I couldn't see being this petty to my sister.

This touches on several attitude issues, the first being who rules the calendar. No bride owns the calendar. Insisting that everyone within your acquaintance not dare schedule their wedding anywhere within a six-month time period labels you as a classic Bridezilla. Equally silly is the notion of "racing" each other to the altar. Who cares? In ten years, no one will even remember the weddings, let alone the anniversaries.

For heaven's sake, crying because your sister plays some stupid game and has a quickie wedding two weeks before your elaborate one? One theme the reader will see throughout this book is the idea that calm, civil brides are very difficult for family and friends to torture with ridiculously petty games and manipulations. We never want to give these people the satisfaction of knowing they have jerked our chain big-time, so we resist the urge to display any emotion that would give away our distress.

Audrey's "baby sister," recognizing that big sis was about to attempt an upstaging maneuver, should have calmly let her carry

The Wedding Consultation

Having recently become engaged and wanting to have a wedding to remember, Brideweena has sought out the services of Miss Jeanne to help her coordinate her wedding. The sum total of Brideweena's wedding knowledge has been acquired from a weekend visit to the library to read back issues of every bridal magazine ever printed and attendance at the weddings of close family and friends. Her best friend Muffin Louise's wedding several months ago will go down in the annals of local history as the most spectacular Bridezilla extravaganza ever to occur in Granville County. Brideweena knows she doesn't want a repeat of that debacle, but also thinks she knows what she wants and how to get it. She needs more professional help than Muffin Louise's offered assistance in planning her wedding.

Miss Jeanne: Hello, welcome to my office. Will you have a seat?

Brideweena: Thank you. I am so glad you are available to coordinate my wedding for me! I am, like, totally stressed out at how much has to be done in the next six months. I have already beaten my head against the wall trying to find chartreuse miniroses for my hairpiece.

Miss Jeanne: I'm glad I can be of assistance. You do understand that the nature of my style of wedding coordinating is to not beat around the bush but rather to tell you all possible consequences of the choices you are considering making. Most wedding coordinators are not going to directly tell you that doing X, Y, and Z will classify you as a first-class Bridezilla, but I believe in telling it like it is. The perfect wedding is one where the newly-weds, the family, the guests, and vendors all walk away marveling at what a wonderful wedding it was. I'm here to give you the wedding of your dreams while preventing mass murder of every relationship you have. Do you think this will work for you?

Brideweena: Oh, yes! Muffin Louise didn't have a wedding coordinator, and believe me, she should have been on some sort of leash. Why I forgave her for putting me through maid-of-honor torture escapes me.

Miss Jeanne: Great! Let's get started. What have you done up to this point?

Brideweena: I have a firm wedding date and I sent out my save-the-date cards a few days ago. Now everyone knows to mark the calendar and I can expect everyone to attend. No excuses for "no shows"!

Miss Jeanne: I think you misunderstood the meaning of the term "save-the-date cards," interpreting them as second-person plural imperative mood—in other words as commands, which they are not.

Brideweena: But everyone who receives a save-the-date card is required to accept the invitation. I will really be peeved if I put all this effort into planning the best wedding ever and people tell me they cannot attend.

Miss Jeanne: Oh, I see [that I am dealing with nascent uncouth behavior that I will have to nip in the bud as soon as possible].

through with it content in the knowledge that her wedding was sufficiently different and reflective of her and her fiancé's tastes. There can be a delicious pleasure in depriving people of the anticipated fruits of their manipulative games while maintaining the dignity to stay above the fray.

Rule 4: It's Rude to Make Comparisons

My story concerns comments made to me by two other couples planning their own weddings. The first was from my brother-in-law: "We want our wedding not to be as formal as George's but definitely better than yours." Our wedding was a simple buffet with hors d'oeuvres, homemade breads, special family dishes, that I'd made myself.

The second comment came just weeks ago from a good friend for whom I will be a bridesmaid at her wedding. She told me that she, too, wanted something more formal and better than our wedding. She is having a barbecue of ribs, chicken, hamburgers, and hot dogs, outside in her parents' small backyard. Apparently barbecue is more formal than homemade hors d'oeuvres, chocolate-dipped fruit, etc.

I guess the lesson to be learned is this: If you're engaged, please use common sense and don't tell someone, "We want our wedding to be better than yours." How rude!

It's really uncouth to tell people you intend to surpass their wedding plans with what you think are infinitely better choices. While it may be tempting to play "Keep up with the Joneses" with your wedding plans, wedding planning isn't yet an Olympic competitive sport.

The only comparison you should be making, quietly to yourself, is that no way on God's green earth are you going to behave like your best friend, Muffin Louise, who morphed into the Bridezilla to beat all Bridezillas when she married.

Rule 5: Rehearsal Dinners . . . Pay Up! Not!

We had been invited to come to the rehearsal to get details on our duties (programs, gift attendees, flower petals, etc.). After a two-hour rehearsal, we drove to a nearby restaurant for dinner. About twenty people were there, including the bride's and groom's parents. Entrees were $12 to $15 each, and we waited forty-five minutes before our order was taken. At the end of the meal, I noticed a line forming at the register of rehearsal dinner guests. Apparently we were supposed to pay for our own dinner! I heard later that one of the ushers paid for the bride and groom, and another usher covered the tab of those who left early, who didn't think they had to pay. We decided that paying for the rehearsal dinner, to the tune of $35, was our wedding gift.

It is becoming an increasing—and annoying—practice to require the bridal party to pay for their own rehearsal dinners or the bridesmaids' luncheon. What with tux rentals, dress and shoe purchases, hair appointments, shower gifts, and travel coming on the bridal party's nickel, you would think the bride and groom or the parents would properly host a rehearsal dinner or bridesmaids' luncheon that does not place yet another financial burden on bridal party members. No wonder people are refusing the "honor" of standing up for a couple's wedding. It's too darned expensive!

Rule 6: Budgeting for the Wedding

Before you can really begin planning a wedding, there is that little matter of money. It's a bit difficult to contract with vendors if you have no idea what your spending limits are. But lack of financial resources has never stopped some people who can devise numerous creative ways to afford a wedding that exceeds their means.

We hear that it is to be a "sponsored" wedding. Tammie does not want to pay for anything, and has convinced Peter that this is the way to go. She claims to be too busy to attend to any details. (What she wants is for someone not to have read her mind so she can rant and blame, but that is another story.) Peter is to call florists, dressmakers, photographers, etc., and convince them to give away their services for free, and they will receive an ad in her wedding program!!!!! Not only that, but my husband is to be the best man, and Tammie has decreed that since he is included in the wedding party, his restaurant "will" provide all of the food for the reception and rehearsal dinner—free. Too bad if he has to leave the wedding to supervise his employees at the reception. And he had better not do that, by the way. He needs to find a way to get it done the "right way." Oh, my God.

The sad part is, Peter has become a lot like her—he is now calling my husband and asking who he has got "to sponsor the bachelor party" and "What airline did you get to pay for our tickets home?"

Both of these people are in their thirties, have professional careers, and come from families of great affluence. I really wonder what on earth is going to happen to this marriage.

Emily Post would be spinning in her grave if she knew weddings were becoming advertising venues. By far the worst solicitation I have ever seen was sent to me by a vendor in Georgia who received a letter from a groom detailing the many "benefits" of sponsoring "Our Wedding":

> Your business name or logo displayed in the announcements, programs, printed on T-shirts and other wedding favors, listed on three Web sites, in the monthly wedding e-mails and newsletters, in the credits listed in the event CD-ROM/VHS tape or DVD movie of the wedding ceremony, signage at the reception venue, on the place cards at the buffet tables and in the table centerpieces, in a published "thank you" in the newspaper; and finally, on the thank-you cards.

Other nefarious methods of accruing cash for a wedding include panhandling Web sites and even eBay auctions. The authors tell piteous tales of overextending their credit or poor income potential that precludes them from getting married. The concept of a simple, affordable wedding either doesn't cross their mind or is summarily ruled out as too plebian for their exalted status. No, what they want is a wedding extravaganza on someone else's dime.

The Web site payforcynthiaswedding.com was one of the worst examples of this genre. Cynthia didn't just want a wedding; she wanted an entire weeklong vacation with rental of a beach house big enough to house the entire wedding party, two limos, her engagement ring and their wedding rings, spa treatments for the bride and her attendants, scuba and Jet Ski rentals for the groom and groomsmen, her wedding gown, buffet dinner and day-after wedding brunch, the wedding party gifts, and the photographer at $4,000 to $6,000. Vendors who donated their services were offered the opportunity to put their logos on various wedding-related paper products. The bottom of the barrel was dredged with the announcement that those donating money would become eligible to win a date with one of the groomsmen.

The Web address went like wildfire through the Internet wedding forums and message boards, resulting in Cynthia's taking down the Web site, claiming that her life and those of her friends and family were being threatened. Probably a bit melodramatic but it does emphasize the fact that people do not appreciate greedy panhandlers even if they are swathed in nuptial white.

But on the heels of those who devise moneymaking schemes to pay for the wedding of their dreams come those who view the wedding solely as a means to a greater financial end.

Rule 7: Money Is the Root of Wedding Evil

In the several months leading up to the wedding, all we heard from the employee was how much money they were going to make from this wedding. He told us, many times, that the only reason he was getting married was because of the money.

A few days before the wedding, a friend of his let my husband and me know that we were expected to give at least $500 as a wedding gift. Well, we really didn't have that sort of money to give. It's not considered culturally appropriate, by the standards of the wider community where we live, to ask for or to give monetary gifts, and it's certainly not considered appropriate to tell guests how much to give. Also, his entire attitude—that he was getting married to make money—bothered us. Instead, we went out and purchased a very nice kitchen appliance that we knew they would need and didn't have for about $100.

It was what we felt we could give. The groom said something to us at the re-
ception about how he really would've preferred cash . . . and of course we never
got a thank-you card or a verbal thank-you.

For weeks after the wedding he complained about how little money he'd
made. Apparently it wasn't enough that his aunt and uncle, who had to travel
halfway around the world at their own expense to be at the wedding, only gave
him $5,000. He thought they should've given more. His parents—who had
financed the entire affair—should've given more. In the end, he was disap-
pointed because he didn't get enough money from the reception for a down pay-
ment on a house, and had to settle for a small apartment instead.

People like this make my skin crawl. The family may feel an obligation to pony up the dough the bride or groom anticipates, but
friends are under no such burden. Upon catching a whiff of that foul
stench of greed, people's wallets tend to shrivel in reaction.

Marriage to them seems to be the best avenue to immediate wealth
accumulation. It doesn't appear at all to be about forming a lasting
commitment with a loving partner. If this is your motivation for marrying, please keep reading this book, as we all hope that you will see
the error of your thinking.

Rule 8: Planning Your Own Parties Is a No-no

Recently my brother threw his own bachelor party. He did this because he felt
his best man was not up to the job. The best man has a reputation for being un-
reliable, so the fact that my brother was throwing his own party was somewhat
overlooked.

The day arrives, and all male friends and relatives attend the golf outing
planned by my brother, which they are expected to pay for on their own. The

crew of men includes three dads since both sets of parents are divorced and all
remarried except for our mother. The golf outing is followed by dinner, which
the guests also have to pay for.

Assuming the role of host or hostess for parties traditionally
hosted by a friend of the family to honor the soon-to-be newlyweds is
a very recent phenomenon. The motivation behind this is a belief that
one is owed a party of a certain caliber and that friends and relations
cannot be trusted to give you the party you think you deserve. So, the
bride or groom take it upon themselves to plan showers, bachelorette
and bachelor parties, and engagement parties for themselves.

Just because you think all your friends are party-planning clods
does not mean you get to take the reins in hand and plan parties in
which you are both the host and guest of honor. I have to wonder if
the storyteller was the best man, and if he wasn't, why didn't *he* host
the bachelor party? So here we have a party in honor of the groom,
planned and hosted by the groom, who then makes his guests pay for
the very party he planned. Tacky beyond belief.

The same goes for the ladies. If you are so unfortunate as to asso-
ciate with close friends who would inflict a male stripper,
phallic-shaped cakes, and that whorish "suck for a buck"
T-shirt on you against your will, you'll just have to live with
the consequences of your life choices. That means either going along with a bachelorette party from hell or having
none at all. It doesn't mean you should throw yourself a
bash and ask others to pay for it.

Brideweena's Checklist

1. Have I got my priorities straight in regard to why I am marrying?

2. Have I made a budget that reflects what I can afford?

3. Have I set my attitude to one of gratitude rather than entitlement?

4. Have I resisted the urge to make vocal comparisons of my wedding to Muffin Louise's, even though her wedding was trashy and ill-mannered?

5. Does my left arm no longer stick out at an abnormal angle with wrist bent to best show off the rock I am wearing?

Attending to the Attendants

Be slow in choosing a friend, but slower
in changing him. —SCOTTISH PROVERB

THE PROPOSAL OF MARRIAGE HAS BEEN ACCEPTED. The families have been notified of your intention to marry. Now it's time to ponder whom you'll ask to stand up for you on your wedding day. Hmmm...decisions, decisions! Should you choose your college drinking buddies who still think barhopping should be an Olympic sport? Or what about that friend you've known since kindergarten but who has since broadened her gluteus maximal horizons? Maybe you should ask your three sisters so you avoid Family World War III. No other area of your wedding planning is as fraught with so many potential opportunities to let loose and give free rein to incivility. Even if you are Saint Brideweena, worthy of the multitudes genuflecting as you process down the aisle, your bridesmaids can still provide you with ample temptation to succumb to the dark side of the Wedding Force.

Rule 1: Be Slow in Choosing Your Attendants

This is a true story about my former best friend. She was getting married to a man who hit on me the night she moved into his house. No lie. Needless to say, many people didn't consider him to be a major "catch."

After their brief courtship led to an engagement, my friend asked me to be her maid of honor. I kept my opinions to myself, and vowed to do the best I could for her.

The first major hurdle was her bridal shower. She had four other brides-maids, all under the age of fifteen (except for one who was getting married her-self and couldn't contribute any money or time). Also, since the bride-to-be's mother wasn't too happy with her choice of husband, she didn't even bother showing up. So all of the planning, production, and finances of the shower were my responsibility. Now, I'm a professional artist, and I don't have a lot of money, but I managed to throw her a heck of a shindig.

When the shower was over, we packed up her car. I offered to put some of her gifts in my car and follow her home, but she insisted on overpacking her car and headed off. A few hours later she called me. . . . Here's how the conversa-tion went:

ME: Hello?

HER: Hey, it's (the bride-to-be).

ME: Oh, hi!

HER: Yeah, where did you get those margarita glasses? (We had a fiesta theme for the bridal shower. I purchased plastic glasses for the party guests, and gave her the margarita stemware she registered for as a shower gift.)

ME: Ummm, I got them at the party store. (Thinking she was referring to the plastic ones.)

HER: (snort) Well, that figures.

I am now totally confused.

HER: They are totally smashed.

(At this point, I understand that she is referring to the glass stemware.)

ME: Oh, those . . . the gift receipt is in the box, you can return them.

HER: Fine, bye.

And she hung up on me.

Now, I may be oversensitive, but I consider that rude. I understand that things get very hectic around the time of your wedding (I just got married myself), but I still managed to be kind to people . . . especially those who went to great lengths for me.

Fast-forward to four weeks before the wedding. My "friend" informs me that her betrothed's bachelor party is now a Jack and Jill. (I guess he couldn't drum up enough friends to attend a party in honor of him.) I am expected to attend the Jack and Jill and pay $25 for the pleasure. The party is two weeks from the time she tells me about it. I gently inform her that I have a spa day with my mother planned that day (which was a Mother's Day present and scheduled two months in advance) and I was a performer in a theater production that night. (With no understudy . . . I really couldn't miss that!) She tells me I have to be there. . . . When I inevitably missed it, I didn't hear from her until the day before the wedding.

One day before her wedding, I offer to do any last-minute tasks and be a support to her in any way. She asked me to pick up an envelope box and said she would see me at the rehearsal the morning of the wedding. And she hung up on me. In the morning, I show up at the rehearsal and she files in with the rest of the bridesmaids, straight from their "bridal sleepover," which I was not invited to attend.

(I guess she was mad I missed her Jack and Jill.) Needless to say, the rest of the day was highly tense.

Now, bear in mind, through all this, I never complained to her and expended every effort to aid her. Even afterward, I kept my opinions to myself.

Three months after her wedding, I wrote her a letter expressing my observation that we had grown apart. I stated that I would understand if she didn't feel comfortable as the matron of honor in my wedding and chose to stand down. (FYI: Girls, never, never promise your friends that they will be your MOH in high school . . . you will regret it later!) She sent a hateful, scathing e-mail to me a month later, stating what a bad friend and awful MOH I was, and she was going to show me how a "real" MOH behaves. After this psychotic episode, I broke etiquette and informed her that she would not be my MOH or an invited guest.

The thing that really eats me is never receiving a thank-you note for the four place settings of her fine china I sent.

Think twice; then think again. Don't make the mistake of getting on the phone to tell everyone of your good fortune and promising your squealing, excited friends that they can share your joy by being bridesmaids. It is never wise to make offers while in the grip of fluttery, just-engaged emotions. You may have to rescind those offers later when you realize you were just a bit too hasty. Once you have made the offer, it is extraordinarily ungracious to rescind it, unless you want a seething friend or sister using your engagement photo as a dartboard. On the other hand, there is nothing ungracious about releasing a friend from an obligation she views as a hardship, as in the case of the above story. Kudos to the storyteller for maintaining her civility and bestowing graciousness on such an undeserving friend!

Rule 2: You Are Not Casting a Theatrical Production

My friend J is getting married next summer. I didn't think I was guaranteed to be an attendant even though we are close. So when I heard I wasn't one I wasn't too upset. Then I have dinner with her the other night and she states how she is struggling to find a fourth attendant. She then goes on to say how she has two heavy attendants and one thin one and they look like two pumpkins in a pea patch. Also two of them are matrons and she really needs a maid. So I am not one because I have the audacity of being married and heavy in weight. I have known her for years and tried to be a good friend to her and kept in touch. But instead she is having someone she hasn't spoken to in years fill the role because she is thin and unmarried.

When choosing bridesmaids, the goal is not to hold each one up for scrutiny and choose the top three based on how well each one fits a specific role. Weddings are not meant to be a theatrical production in which parts are created and cast according to talent or physical suitability. When the temptation to create the perfectly orchestrated, one-day extravaganza hits, it tantalizes a bride to use people as cast members at the expense of relationships. It becomes too easy to size up friends and family as to how well they will fit the parts and discard those whose physical assets are deemed inferior.

Tara let it slip that she had originally asked girls from her college dorm to be her attendants, but had kicked them out of the wedding party because they were "too fat, and she wanted good pictures."

Often the flimsy excuse I hear from brides for being too discriminating in their choice of attendants is that they are paying a premium price for photography and they want lovely photographs that will last forever. In this shortsighted perspective, overweight or unattractive attendants would mar that perfect wedding album.

For shame if this thought flitted across your mind! Heaps of disdain if you actually apply these cruel criteria for your attendants. While wedding photography is expensive, it is a mark of self-absorption to weigh the value of friendship against a $1,800 photography album and find the photography more valuable. People who inflict this prioritization on friends deserve a cold place in Etiquette Hell, all cuddled up with their precious photo albums, for the petty and superficial treatment of that rare commodity known as "friendship."

Rule 3: You Are Not in Charge of Family Planning for Your Attendants

My husband's best friend was getting married and to my surprise the bride-to-be asked me to be her maid of honor (my husband was the best man). She knew when she asked me to be in the wedding that we were planning on having a third child, but we were looking to buy a house soon and were waiting until we moved to get pregnant. The bride actually told me a year before the wedding that I couldn't be pregnant for Her wedding. One or two months pregnant was all right, but she didn't want me showing for the wedding.

Being the bride does not give one dictatorial powers to intrude on people's lives and expect them to alter their reproductive schedules just to suit your notion of what a perfect wedding should look like. It is the height of maniacal tyranny to presume everyone else's lives must go on hold so that the bride's wedding is not "marred" by the presence of a pregnant attendant! I've seen a bridesmaid as pregnant as eight and a half months; her relationship to the bride was so close that not having the expectant mother in attendance would have seemed odd.

However, you should be concerned that a bridesmaid could be so close to her due date that her participation in your wedding would be an added burden to her. But the decision as to whether she can fulfill her obligations is hers to make, not yours. Ask, but be certain also to express concern that she be comfortable, thus giving her a gracious "out" if she needs to decline the offer but is worried you might be offended that she cannot accept.

Rule 4: The Number of Attendants Is Not Important

One day, Lynn and Tim came up to the apartment, and announced that they were getting married. Yippee. Lynn told me, even though I was supposedly her best friend, that she was not sure if I would be in the wedding, since she had asked her sister, two mutual friends of ours, and Tim's sister. Tim simply had very few friends, so it was hard for him to think of anyone else to match me up with, and she was unsure if I could be in it or not. Okay, I played like it was no big deal, but to me, here is a girl I grew up with and had been best friends with since, like, third grade. I was hurt . . . not only by the fact that I was her roommate, but by the fact that now we even had two mutual friends that apparently rated higher than me on the eligibility scale.

A couple weeks later, Lynn says Tim has asked another "friend" from the grocery store he works at to stand up for him so I am "in." Yippee.

It is not imperative that there be a specific number of attendants. Formal etiquette divas will explain that the formality level of a wedding dictates the number of attendants—the more formal the wedding, the greater the number of attendants. This silly notion needs to be ditched like a 1970s pink ruffled tuxedo shirt in favor of choosing attendants who hold a special place in the groom's and bride's hearts.

The Wedding Consultation

Brideweena: My friends are so dear to me. I just can't think of how I will choose between them all! Would it be too tacky if I have fifteen bridesmaids while my groom only has three groomsmen?

Miss Jeanne: Disparity in the number of bridesmaids versus groomsmen is not an etiquette issue regardless of what your mother says. It does cause some logistical issues of how they will process and recess down the aisle, but if that is the worst problem you have in your wedding planning, count your blessings! However, with that many bridesmaids, I can guarantee that your wedding guests' attention will be diverted to counting how many people are standing up at the front of the altar and how much money the bridal shop made on your wedding, and not how lovely you look. Your guests will not be gasping breathlessly at your splendor; they will be agog at the endless parade of attendants. "Good grief, Martha, how many are there up there?" Not to mention the visual impact of twenty backsides facing the congregation. Do you really want to embed that imagery into your guests' minds?

Another thing to consider is that as the number of attendants increases, the statistical odds that there will be more conflict among the bridesmaids or with you increases exponentially. As the bride, you will be called upon to settle disputes, misunderstandings, and conflicts among them. Are you ready to assume leadership of fifteen women who may, or may not, be hormonally jiving with each other?

Brideweena: Twenty backsides, did you say?

Often the worst culprits in perpetuating this false rule are mothers of the bride who have a certain expectation of what they think a daughter's wedding should look like. A few guests have also had the audacity to e-mail me stories of mismatched or unequal numbers of attendants, hoping I'll concur with them that this is tacky. Far from it!

I hear repeatedly of wedding attendants who were chosen solely to fill a vacant attendant slot since their relationship to the bride or groom was somewhat distant. For some brides trying to fill the quota, any warm body that is breathing and has a passing acquaintance with her is potential bridesmaid material. Coworkers may seem like possible candidates, but if you have no further social interaction with them beyond the confines of your work cubicle, strongly resist the urge to ask your officemates to stand up for you. There are consequences to asking marginally close people to be attendants. These include an increased likelihood of miscommunication, disinterest, backing out at the last minute, and more backstabbing than at a convention of Ginsu knife salesmen.

Rule 5: Social Paybacks Are Not Required

When I was a senior in college, I got engaged to my boyfriend of four years. About a week after the announcement, my friend Candice announced her engagement to the guy she had been seeing for about six months. We each asked the other to be in our weddings.

I began planning my wedding, which was to take place in a year and a half. I wanted to have a wedding that our friends and family would truly enjoy.

My parents paid for the reception and open bar, but I wanted to pay for things like flowers, a band, and other special things that I thought my guests would enjoy. In order to pay for these extra touches, I bartended full-time while completing my degree. And scrimped and saved to make it happen.

At the same time, Candice began planning a wedding that would take place in a year. She informed me that it was to be a destination wedding, and they would be getting married on a cruise ship. As her plans unfolded, I found out that we would be expected to pay for transportation, accommodations, our attire, and of course I would get them a gift. I figured it would cost over a thousand dollars all together. I was expected to be down there on Friday for the rehearsal and the wedding would take place on Saturday, and I would then have to hop on a plane to come back home because I still had classes on Monday and would have to skip classes on Friday to attend. Please don't think I begrudge anybody having the wedding of their dreams, but she told me that the reason they were having the wedding this way was to save money, because it would only cost them about $200 above the cost of their cruise to put the wedding on (the groom's parents paid for the cruise). I was told that the parents of the bride had offered to pay for a large wedding and reception, but they had given the couple the option to keep the cash, which they took. I anguished over the decision, but finally came to the conclusion that with saving for my wedding, I could not afford to attend. I told Candice, and said that although I couldn't be at the wedding, I would love to throw her a shower. She said she understood, and that a lot of people weren't going to be able to come, including her own brother and sister and the groom's brother.

The day of the shower rolls around. I get up at five in the morning, after working late the night before, to cook and set up the shower. In my opinion, everything was beautiful and a lot of people told me they thought so, too. Most of the people at the shower were not going to be able to attend the wedding, and at one point the groom's mother expressed to me that they weren't very happy about the location and planning of the wedding, and they were planning a large reception after the couple got back so that they could invite all the people who were not able to be at the wedding. The MOH did not make it to the shower because she said she had hurt her back.

They had planned the bachelorette party for after the shower. The MOH calls and says she can't get transportation down there, and can we pick her up in the limo? (It's an hour to where she lives, and an hour back.) I guess her back had healed since that morning, and now she was ready to party. I suggest since they are going to be two hours, that I go home and change. (I was dressed for a shower and not clubbing, and the other girls had changed at the bride's house.) My apartment was right on the way when they were coming back, so they could pick me up. That was okay with the bride.

I go home, shower, get dressed, do my hair and makeup. They call me from the maid of honor's house, and say they decided to have dinner up there (the plan was to pick me up and then have dinner), so it will be a little longer until they pick me up. I sit there and wait. And wait. And wait. I wait about five hours, and fall asleep on the couch. They call me at about midnight, saying they are on the way back, and should be able to pick me up in about forty-five minutes. They are extremely drunk, and I am sober and very, very tired. I would have to change clothes, and fix my hair and makeup that got messed up when I fell asleep. I tell them I am very sorry, but I am not up to going out. I did feel really bad about it.

The next afternoon, I called to apologize to the bride, and see how the party went. She screams at me that she no longer wants to be my friend, not because of the bachelorette party fiasco, but apparently she is very angry that I wasn't going to be able to make it to her wedding, and didn't want to be my friend anymore. Hmmm, I really wish she had told me that before I spent $300 throwing her a shower, and bought her a nice gift. I haven't had any contact with her since that day (including, of course, any type of thank-you note).

A frequently heard reason for choosing a bridesmaid is the false belief that there is a social obligation to return the favor. Just because someone asked you to stand up for her in her wedding does not mean you are obliged to invite her to be your wedding attendant. I've heard from numerous brides who, against their better judgment, asked a friend to be an attendant just because they had been in the friend's wedding. Ultimately they regretted this decision. The downside of not reciprocating the honor of bridesmaid selection is that the first bride may be surprised and even offended that the relationship is not at the level she thought it was. This revelation may require a bit of diplomacy and kindly fence-mending, but it does not justify putting your wedding plans at risk or your other relationships in peril. Making someone a bridesmaid doesn't make her a close friend. Pretending the relationship is more than it is won't help if there are strains down the road. Why subject yourself and your other attendants to the falseness and the risks? Better to be honest, though kind about it, and safe.

Rule 6: Thou Shalt Not Burden Thy Attendants' Wallets and Goodwill

Mary's wedding, for which I was the maid of honor, was the single most hellish experience of my life. I had to put up with Mary's tacky and thoughtless demands, her utter disregard for the monetary limitations of friends and family, and her need to be in control of every little situation. The night before and the day of the wedding will always stand out in my mind as the worst days of my life. Mary screamed at everyone in her wedding party constantly and almost drove me to tears more than once. It was a challenge for us bridesmaids to keep from strangling her. All in all, with the parties, gifts, dress and tux rentals, and makeup and shoes, my fiancé and I dropped close to a thousand dollars on Mary's wedding.

As this storyteller relates, it *is* expensive to accept the position of wedding attendant. A bridesmaid's willingness to expend considerable amounts of money to honor you with her support should not be exploited. The cost of being a bridesmaid keeps rising, with the average total costs of gifts, attire, transportation, and showers now reaching as much as $1,000. Some wedding-planning guides suggest that you not even bother asking a potential bridesmaid to stand up for you if you believe she cannot financially afford the "honor." I consider it presumptively rude to speculate on someone's private financial health and make an exclusionary conclusion based on that speculation. Doing so certainly can lead to misunderstanding and hurt feelings when friends fail to understand the reason why they were not chosen while someone else was, particularly if your speculation about their means was incorrect. As the bride, you have to walk a fine line between choosing bridesmaids who are able to commit to the requirements of being attendants, yet not choosing bridesmaids based solely on their financial health so they can fulfill your dream-wedding fantasies.

A major area of misunderstanding, and therefore conflict, with bridesmaids is who pays for what. Sometimes there is a presumption that bridesmaids should know the obligations and responsibilities of being a bridesmaid. Very often, they do not. Bridesmaids have been known to accept the honor of attending a bride but having no clue as to how much this honor will set them back. When the cash register starts chinging, the tension starts mounting. Even worse, some brides don't even bother telling their hapless friends of the impending financial brick about to drop on them until it is too late for the attendant to bow out gracefully. This is an extremely awkward position in which to put someone.

You should carefully evaluate what your budget for the wedding

The Wedding Consultation

Brideweena: So, who pays for what? I'm not made of money either!"

Miss Jeanne: The following chart will clear up the ambiguity of who has what financial responsibilities.

Attendants' expense responsibilities for themselves:

- Gift for bride/groom

- Shower or luncheon for bride or bachelor party for groom

- Apparel and accessories
- Transportation costs if out of town

Bride's/groom's expense responsibilities for bridal party:

- Lodging and food expenses if attendants are from out of town
- Transportation to the ceremony and to the reception
- Gifts for attendants

Brideweena: Does "apparel and accessories" include hairstyling and cosmetics? I want all my bridesmaids in swept-up hairstyles with matching Romantic Blush nail polish on nails and toes.

Miss Jeanne: If you want the bridesmaids in matching updo hairstyles, designer cosmetics, and pristinely manicured nails, the obligation for paying for that expense should fall to you, the bride. There is nothing wrong with letting the bridesmaids wear their hair and makeup in the most flattering styles for each of them. What a novel idea in this age of cookie-cutter bridesmaids!

Brideweena (pouting): And to think I forked over $150 at Muffin Louise's insistence to have my hair, makeup, and nails done at OhLaLa Salon.

party will be and communicate that to your potential attendants. Under no circumstances are you to communicate your expectations of what they are to pay for a gift for you or what you think they should spend on your shower. *Mucho* tacky!

If you really wish to have someone stand with you on your wedding day, but it becomes evident that she has limited means to do so, consider discreetly assisting her financially. Perhaps you can chip in on her dress, or arrange transportation for her, or such. You could offer to pay for all wedding-party attire, which would earn you the adoring admiration of your friends as a truly generous person. You could just make private arrangements with the attendants least able to afford the honor. (And make sure this is kept private since you could face jealousy if your other attendants find out.) Just consider it part of the cost of the perfect celebration of your marriage of which you've always dreamed. After all, what is more valuable, a few extra flowers or the presence of your beloved friend?

Once your attendants have committed copious quantities of hard-earned cash to participate in your wedding, it is imperative not to abuse them, since they have accepted the dubious honor of standing up for you. They didn't pay for the privilege of being your personal whipping boys while you have a stress-induced, ego-satisfying scream-o-rama on your wedding day. Just bear this in mind as you continue to plan the rest of your wedding: Never presume that the absence of negative feedback means your behavior is acceptable or forgiven. Silence does not bespeak attendants who are happily tolerating verbal abuse and presumptions on their generosity. If you behave like a fire-breathing harpy, you cannot always expect your attendants to tell you to your face what a heinous monstrosity you have become. Why should they, when there is real potential for their being charred to a cinder? Instead, you may find yourself merrily reading about other people's wedding faux pas on www.etiquettehell.com and stumble on one that sounds distressingly similar to your own wedding. Busted!

Rule 7: Graciously Accept It if a Friend Declines to Be a Bridesmaid

When I first got engaged I knew right away I wanted my oldest and dearest friend to be a bridesmaid. We had talked about it since childhood. I also decided to ask a cousin who had been a close friend of mine for quite a while. They both agreed to be in the wedding and seemed thrilled to be asked.

A year and a half later when the shower was to come around, hosted by an old friend of the family, I told the bridesmaids about it. They had no expenses, only to be there and enjoy the day. My oldest and dearest friend informed me, barely over a month before the wedding, that she couldn't afford to be in the wedding and had to drop out. I was crushed. Between the dresses, which I had made, and the shoes, the cost was about $60. I bit my tongue and told her that I understood but I still wanted her to please attend the shower and wedding— it meant a lot to me.

If a friend declines the offer of being a bridesmaid, accept it graciously. While it is tempting to speculate on the reasons why she isn't leaping for joy at your engagement and salivating at the chance to be a bridesmaid, it's best just to let it go and continue the search. Some women have the dubious pleasure of being a bridesmaid multiple times, sometimes in the same year, and it gets tiring as well as financially draining. If she declines, it may be that she would prefer to enjoy celebrating your wedding as a guest rather than accept the position of bridesmaid with all its attendant responsibilities.

If you receive more than two demurrals, or if attendants start quitting in mid–wedding planning, start taking a hard look at yourself, your wedding costs, and your relationship to these people. Your friends might be sending you a subtle signal that there is no way on earth they would be a bridesmaid to someone they see morphing into a Bridezilla.

Rule 8: Do Not Inflict a Fashion Atrocity on Your Bridesmaids

Once you have completed the casting list, er . . . um, selected the attendants for your wedding, you next get to experience the joys of finding a bridesmaid dress that pleases the varied fashion preferences of all your attendants. Once the bridesmaid dress of your dreams has been swathed across the smorgasbord of sizes, and the reality of bulges in the wrong places has smacked face-to-face with your dream of everyone in sleek, fashionable sheaths, you have the character-building opportunity to replace fantasy with reality and learn the adult life skill of compromise.

The bride had selected a local seamstress to make the dress and told me where to go to get my measurements taken. She had explained what she wanted and all we needed to do was show up for three fittings and then pay for our dresses when they were done. Cool. I had never been in a wedding before, but to me, whatever the bride wanted was cool with me. Little did I know.

I went in for my first measurements, no problem. Second fitting comes around . . . well, there is something close to one dress done hanging on a hanger. I could tell that it was going to be a disaster. The thick straps went over the shoulders . . . the whole underneath of the dress was white. The waist was dropped down to the hips in a not very flattering style and then from there hung to the ground. Over the top of the white material was a very bright baby blue netting. UGH . . . terrible, but this was what she wanted, so more power to her. At the second fitting I had to pay the seamstress a hundred bucks, the rest payable on receipt of the dress.

About a week before the wedding I had my final fitting, even though the dress wasn't totally finished. I had to pay the rest of the money for it, $150! Which was outrageous. I have seen dresses comparable in the Disney Store . . . it looked like a costume. I paid 250 bucks for the ugliest dress in the world. I was angry, but then again, what could I do? On Thursday before the wedding on Saturday the groom comes into the store I work at and informs me, "Lorna hates the dresses. You guys have to get new ones." I am like, "WHAT???!!" She had never even been in to look at them the whole time. Two days to go and she is rejecting them. We live in a small rural town, as well, so there is no way to get everyone together and take them to the closest mall, which is several hours away, and a few of the bridesmaids are not easy-to-find sizes. Turns out the seamstress does a quick fix on the dresses to supposedly make them better and we all have to buy a hoop skirt to wear underneath them. Apparently, that is supposed to make them better.

Later on during the reception, the dresses ripped right off our bodies as we danced. Our friend Gina had her whole side midriff seam ripped out . . . so you could see her side and bra. She had to wear a coat most of the evening.

This story exemplifies the fact that even if you choose the most god-awful bridesmaid dress, your attendants will gamely go along with the fashion massacre in a mistaken allegiance to bridal tyranny while inwardly seething that you are inflicting this on them. No one wants to tell the bride that her dress choice is an abomination for the eyes any more than people were willing to tell the emperor parading in his new "clothes" that he was naked! Their reluctance also has a foundation in the fear that when a bride is faced with the indisputable reality that her dream dress really is a nightmare, she may "kill the messenger." I've been the recipient of dozens of stories in which a bridesmaid or maid of honor tells of having been summarily and casually dismissed from the wedding party by the bride for daring to even appeal the choice of dress. The message the bride sent was loud and clear: "Snap into line, wear what I tell you, or you are out of here, you traitor to my glorious wedding!" There are consequences to speaking up to Bridezilla.

An attendant should not be faulted for trying to dissuade the bride

The Wedding Consultation

Brideweena: My mother says I have to have the exact same bridesmaid dresses or the wedding will look tacky.

Miss Jeanne: Why have exactly matching dresses anyway? The cookie-cutter bridesmaid look is soo boring and passé! There are creative ways to individualize your wedding and have happy bridesmaids too.

Same dress, different colors, letting each bridesmaid choose what color looks best for her.

Different dresses, same color, again letting bridesmaids choose what flatters them best. To get an exact color match, have the bridesmaids choose dresses from within one designer's line. This way you get a continuity of design style yet different dresses while preserving the same color. One bride I know simply gave the bridesmaids a color swatch and told them to have fun choosing a full-length, formal gown of their own preference.

One innovative solution a bride had was to give her attendants yards of the same fabric and let them have a dress made in the fashion each felt looked best on her.

Brideweena: Whew! Mom does not know it all!

from a bridesmaid dress that would not flatter all her bridesmaids. The kind and gracious bride listens to even the subtle messages coming from her bridesmaids regarding her choice of attendant apparel and considers her friendships of greater importance than her dream vision of the perfect bridesmaid dress. Do you really want to be known as the kind of person who would subject her supposedly dearest friends to the humiliation of wearing an absolute atrocity? Or worse, someone who values a dress more highly than a relationship?

Rule 9: Do Not Commit Bridesmaidicide if They Hate the Dress They Originally Told You They Loved

Last summer, about six weeks before she got married, my friend Martha asked me to be in her wedding party, as she couldn't rely on her maid of honor to do anything and was afraid of getting stuck. I was thrilled, and because her husband, Thomas, was in our wedding party already, I asked if she would return the favor and be in our wedding too.

The next several weeks flew by, and I met the other girls in the wedding party, and they chose the dress we were going to wear, with absolutely no input from me, and basically pretended I didn't exist on the dress-buying expedition. They picked out a dress that looked hideous on all three of us and cost nearly two hundred dollars, but because it was not my wedding and the bride seemed happy, I just bit my tongue and went along with it.

When it came time to purchase the dresses for my wedding, I told all three of my girls that I didn't care what dress they chose, so long as they could come to a mutual decision and they were all happy with it. We went shopping and they tried on dresses and chose a dress that was flattering to them all (all three of my bridesmaids have completely different body types, so this was a chore!) and it was not terribly expensive, either.

About a month later, we met Martha and Thomas for lunch, and the first thing out of Thomas's mouth when we sat down to eat was, "Well, I guess you finally got your payback with the bridesmaid dress after what Martha made you wear!" I was shocked. Martha stammered out something about how much she didn't hate the dress, but I could tell she hates it. I still can't figure out why she went along with it, knowing that I didn't really care too much what they wore!

Sometimes you can do everything right and still someone hates the dress and is offended they have to wear it. If you've been as gracious as possible and given the bridesmaids the opportunity to express their dissatisfaction with the dress choice and your willingness to change, you've done the best you can do. You will not please everyone, and there will be situations in which, no matter what you do, someone is an unhappy camper. At those times, you have to fall back on the knowledge that you were as fair as possible to everyone and just let it go. Being civil does not mean you are a doormat nor does it require that you beat yourself with guilt.

Rule 10: Do Not Obsess Over Little Things

Right before the pictures, Nora demanded that everyone remove their jewelry. I was the only one who had a problem with this, because my fiancé had given me a small necklace with a heart-shaped pendant on it and asked me not to take it off until we were married. I explained this to her and offered to turn it around backward so that it wouldn't show, but noooooo . . . this was not good enough and she started screaming at me that I was ruining her wedding. Her mother told me that if I didn't take that necklace off, I wouldn't be in the wedding. I politely refused and said if she would rather I not be in the wedding, that was fine. After much fuss, and some really dirty looks from the mother of the bride and her sisters, I was reluctantly allowed to be in the wedding.

And the moral of the story is . . . the bride's wedding wasn't ruined! Who would have thought that an ounce of gold chain could have had such devastating effects on the emotional stability of not only the bride, but all the female members of her family, as well!

Like Dracula when he sees garlic, some brides recoil into writhing wretches when an object crosses their visual path that violates their ban on contraband attendant wear. It could be a necklace, a different panty-hose color than that of the other bridesmaids, different nail polish (or none when it was ordered that there will be), or a hairstyle that was not on the bride's approved list. These are just some of the petty tarradiddle with which an obnoxious bride may be tempted to torture her friends and family, throwing a full-fledged tantrum just before the ceremony. One woman told me how her future sister-in-law threw a royal screamfest of a tantrum within earshot of all the guests when she realized one of the groomsmen, soon to be a brother-in-law, had not cut his hair short *enough* for her tastes. Don't think for a moment that such behavior will be overlooked and have no relational consequences.

If you do not have unrealistic and demanding expectations of what your attendants should look like right down to the eyelash, you will be far less likely to blow a gasket when someone or something doesn't quite look perfect to you. There is more to life, and more to a wedding day, than obsessing over jewelry or any other fluff that wouldn't show up in a wedding photo except with a magnifying glass. It is utterly ridiculous to think anyone else even remotely cares if one attendant has a different shoe style or a different nail polish or hair a tad too long. Get a grip!

An old friend from college asked me to be in his wedding last summer. We had not seen each other for two years, but had e-mailed news to each other so I knew he was engaged. The tux I had to rent was a standard, double-breasted one. I know I have a slight "gut" and look better in a single, but who was I going to argue with on this? So I plunked down $95 for the rental.

Comes the day of the wedding and I see the bridesmaids in their gowns all standing around the bride's room at the church looking upset. It seems one of them is pregnant and her gown no longer fits well enough for the bride to accept. The bride decided to remove the pregnant bridesmaid from the wedding just one hour before the wedding is to start. All of the bridesmaids are a little shocked at this, but are trying to put on the best face they can.

The groom and the rest of us guys all go into the room designated for us to use to change and get ready. Twenty minutes later, the bride knocks on the door and walks in to "inspect" us. She looks at all of us then grabs the groom and pulls him aside. After a rather heated discussion, during which we can hear her say, "He is the fattest and looks the worst," she walks out and the groom asks to talk to me privately. It seems the bride has decided that there cannot be a difference in the number of attendants, so she decided I (as the obviously largest of the group) had to go.

The groom said he was sorry, but couldn't do anything about it. I told him that I thought he and the bride should be ashamed of themselves for treating people like this after what the bridesmaid and I had paid for our clothing, and after we had spent time and money to travel to the wedding, and had done so because we cared about the two of them. I further said that if our physical appearances were going to be the reason for our being in or out of the wedding, then friendship obviously didn't matter too much. He shrugged his shoulders and said that he was going to do whatever she wanted, so I was going to have to leave.

Needless to say, I did not attend the wedding or the reception and I kept the gift I had brought for them. To this day, I have not heard a word from him or his new wife.

This is such a tragic story, I almost want to don sackcloth and ashes in mourning! Several friendships destroyed because of the bride's skewed priorities and the groom's lack of backbone to stand up for what is right. Was the "perfect" wedding of one day worth the sacrifice of years of relationship? Apparently for this bride, it was. Double shame on her!

The groomsman is to be commended for his refusal to go along with the bride's edict. He appealed to the groom, whose lack of spinal fortitude sacrificed a long-standing friendship on the altar of his bride's demands. Once out of the heat of wedding-day stress, this bride and groom may have experienced profound shame at their behavior, but the damage done is irreparable.

It was bad enough that the bride ditched a pregnant bridesmaid minutes before the wedding ceremony, but uneven numbers of attendants was not a sufficient reason to reduce the number of groomsmen. There is no etiquette mandate that requires an even number of attendants and there is certainly no civil way to "fire" an attendant right before the wedding on such baseless grounds. The cosmic harmony of nature will not be tossed into cataclysmic imbalance if there is one more groomsman, even two more, than there are bridesmaids.

The Wedding Consultation

Brideweena: Okay, the mental picture of twenty backsides facing my guests is rather daunting, but even if I cut my number of bridesmaids down to a reasonable level, how do I handle the different number of groomsmen?

Miss Jeanne: A wedding ceremony does not have to be an elaborately choreographed pas de deux between groomsmen and bridesmaids as they trip the light fantastic down the church aisle. There is nothing wrong with two groomsmen or two bridesmaids walking side by side during a processional or one bridesmaid flanked on each side by two groomsmen.

Brideweena: I know I'll hurt someone's feelings by not having her be a bridesmaid so are there any other jobs I can give her instead?

Miss Jeanne: Certainly! A well-planned wedding can offer numerous opportunities for friends and family to fill positions of special honor or service. Here is a list of some: vocalist, reader, program dispenser, guest-book attendant, usher, cake server, punch pourer, and so on.

Brideweena: Punch pouring! Oh, yeah, I can just see my Yuppie Princess college roommate doing that!

Miss Jeanne: In some areas of the South, it is considered an honor to serve the punch. I've seen wrinkled, little, old Southern biddies fighting like barnyard hens for the privilege. In addition, the punch pourer can be the first line of defense against your groom's frat friends spiking it with something a bit more interesting, or Uncle Charlie who doesn't think it is a wedding reception without his famous "moon juice" added to the punch.

Rule 11: If You Have to "Fire" an Attendant, Be Gracious About It

When I was in college a friend of mine, whom we shall call Penelope, asked me to be in her wedding. I was very excited and accepted. In the spring before the wedding, I saw the dress I was supposed to get, but we had not gotten an order form yet. Over the summer, I e-mailed her continuously to try to get information on the wedding, the dress, etc. In the fall, she avoided me and finally I asked one of the other girls if I was still in the wedding and she said that I wasn't. I was in shock since Penelope had never mentioned it to me. When she found out I knew she said she didn't want me in the wedding because I was too opinionated and she thought I might upset her on her wedding day! I couldn't believe it! I felt so rejected, especially since she didn't have the guts to tell me herself. One of my other friends told me I had to go to the wedding so that I could save face and I did. I tried to be as nice as possible, but to this day we are still not friends.

Although rare, sometimes the need arises to divest the bridal party of an attendant. The way this is executed will stand as testimony to your priorities, kindness, and character, so tread carefully. You had best ponder long and hard whether the offense is serious enough to warrant the action of termination. Once you "fire" an attendant, you can kiss that relationship good-bye, because it is nearly impossible to mend that relational fence.

In this particular situation, I truly do not believe the bride had a justifiable excuse for firing the bridesmaid. The fundamental assumption in asking friends to stand up for you is that there is a relationship that can survive the ups and downs that are inevitable in interactions with people. It is unlikely the bridesmaid suddenly became "too opinionated." Rather, the bride had an epiphany one day and decided that this particular quality in her friend was not advantageous on her wedding day. What was previously tolerated during the course of friendship became an intolerable obstacle for the wedding day. If you were too hasty in choosing your bridesmaids and you are now wallowing in a whole heap of regret, it's time to embrace the consequences of your actions and suck it up. Being mature enough to marry means that you are mature enough to honor your commitments to relationships first. Once you open your mouth and utter those five words, "Will you be my bridesmaid," you've set the invitation in stone. You should be loath to retract your verbal commitment over anything less than truly abominable behavior.

What are the actions that would qualify a bridesmaid or groomsman to be demoted? Clearly, illegal activities—like drug use—or an inability to stay sober. A persistent pattern of nastiness would do it, as evidenced by snide comments, sabotage of the relationship (like soliciting your groom), persistent opposition to wedding plans, as shown by not returning repeated phone calls or stating a refusal to attend the rehearsal. Would the behavior your attendant is engaging in be sufficient to terminate a friendship if it were not connected to your wedding planning? If it is and you have no intention of ever speaking with your "friend" again in your lifetime, fire her now rather than go through a pantomime of civility during the wedding-day celebrations, knowing you intend to cut her out of every wedding photo afterward.

Too many brides want to fire an attendant for self-serving reasons such as not organizing a bridal shower. However, her being a party-planning clod is not sufficient reason to hatchet the maid of honor from the wedding-party ranks. Not making a dress deposit in a timely manner, cutting hair so that the hair ornament no longer fits, getting pregnant, or incurring your fiancé's dislike are not sufficient reasons for dismissal either. Your groom is also under an obligation to honor relationship commitments and he should not be placing you in the awkward position of having to "choose" between him and your friends.

If a bridesmaid deserves to be fired, do it as forthrightly, as unemotionally, and as soon as possible. A personal face-to-face discussion is essential, since you are about to terminate a friendship. Such an action should never be trivialized with a dismissive voice mail or e-mail. This is not the time to scream recriminations or accusations. On the other hand, avoiding the problem or putting it off, as the bride did in the above story, is very rude and cowardly. Waiting until the last possible minute to inform her bridesmaid was doubly cruel and exposed her to unnecessary embarrassment. Once face-to-face with the troublesome bridesmaid, explain that while you are sorry that things have come to this point, it has become necessary to release her from her obligations. Return any wedding-related gifts she may have given you and wish her well.

Sometimes a prospective bridesmaid really does not want to endure the dress shopping and fittings, the expenses, and the obligations that go with being a bridesmaid, but she does not have the heart to tell you plainly that she would rather not accept the position. Some people do not know how to say no without feeling terribly awkward. They may accept your offer to be an attendant and then subsequently drag their feet and appear listless about your wedding planning as a form of passive-aggressive resistance. If you suspect this may be the case, the appropriate solution is to approach your bridesmaid in person and gently explain that you understand that her life is busy and that perhaps the demands of being a brides-maid are too much for her at this moment. Assure her that you would understand completely and would not harbor any hard feelings if she prefers to bow out. This graciously gives her an "out" to save face and dignity yet preserves the friendship. She may accept the offer or she may not, protesting that she is excited and wants to participate. Give her some time to think about it and reaffirm your appreciation of her regardless of her decision.

As noted above, these rules are not the only ones, but they are the most common ones broken by the denizens of Etiquette Hell, whom I hope you will not join. Other situations with your bridesmaids will present themselves and thus present opportunities to act graciously with civility and kindness. If you approach these problem situations asking yourself, "Have I treated him or her with respect? Have I pre-sumed upon them in any way? Am I grateful for what they have done for me?" the answers you derive will lead you in choosing to act civilly regardless of how unusual the situation may be.

Remember that your wedding day may be the most beautiful day of your life, but the real beauty of your life will be in the relationships that last far longer than a day. Make sure your wedding planning and wedding day enhance your friendships and set the stage for a lifetime of love, both with your husband and with those who have lovingly stood with you on that special day.

Brideweena's Checklist

1. Have I chosen my bridesmaids on the basis of my relationship to them and not superficial criteria of appearance or social obligation?

2. Have I given them enough information as to what to expect, i.e., they will need to pay for their dresses but I'll pay for the shoes, etc.?

3. Have I taken into consideration their thoughts on what dress style would look best on them?

4. Have I thought through the consequences of having more than a few attendants?

5. Have I presumed to believe all my attendants will happily pay for hair appointments, dyeable shoes, nail manicures, dress alterations, and travel to attend my wedding?

6. Have I bought suitable attendant gifts?

THREE

Issuing the Invitations

I must decline your invitation owing to a
subsequent engagement. —OSCAR WILDE

*E*NGRAVING OR THERMOGRAPHY? Lithography or laser printing? If you think your etiquette karma is dependent on which
method of printing you choose for the invitations, you have
been sadly deluded by false misconceptions carried over from a by-
gone era. I remember when etiquette rules dictated that anything less
than engraved invitations represented a social faux pas that displayed
your fall from high society. But were guests really fondling the invitations a little too intimately and snootily appraising the host's social
status based on whether the lettering was raised enough to the touch?
Who knows, but who would want such obsessive-compulsive snobs at
her wedding anyway?

People today aren't easily offended by such issues as the printing
methods or paper weight of the invitations they receive. In all of Etiquette Hell's existence, not one of the thousands of stories submitted
has ever addressed someone's offense at receiving a laser-printed invitation when they thought an engraved one was necessary. What of-

fends people are the goofs, the sloppiness, the presumptions, and the blatant begging for money.

The invitation is a vital first clue to guests regarding the style and formality of the event to which they are being invited. You don't send formal invitations to a good ol' boy pig-pickin' wedding reception where blue jeans are the uniform of the day. Likewise, you don't fake out your guests with cutesy cartoon characters on the invitation when the event requires formal evening wear at the Grand Poobah Hotel.

Most etiquette books will go into boring detail as to the exact science of a "most formal" invitation. All those details can become more important than the substance. Does it really matter that a "most formal" invitation uses British spelling such as "honour" and "favour"? Probably not to your guests. However, the goal of a formal invitation is to set the tone for how *you* view your wedding. Therefore sending a formal invitation can express the level of importance and substance you are giving the event. It sounds trite, but attention to such details as not abbreviating titles, writing out dates, and using proper wording can be viewed by guests as a measure of how we approach one of life's most momentous events. It won't hurt you to be fussy about these details.

Immutable Fact of Life

The invite contained a typed insert with hotel details and directions to the church and venue. I stopped counting at twelve typographical errors and two blobs of Tippex (British for what I think you call Wite-Out).

It will hurt you to be a slob about spelling because, like it or not, the impression people will receive is that you are putting very little care into this extension of hospitality. They may then conclude that this will translate into carelessness about the whole wedding. Sorry if that grates against your sensibilities, but it's human nature to believe "sloppy is as sloppy does."

Rule 1: Nearer My Heart to Thee, Please

This happened to me just a few months ago. I opened my mailbox one day to find a very nice wedding invitation envelope. I thought it strange since I wasn't aware of anyone in my circle of family or friends getting married. The bafflement increased when I opened and read the invitation—I had no idea who this couple was! I thought that surely they must have sent me the invitation by mistake. But no, my correct name and address were on the address label. I still am not sure what happened, but the only identifiable thing I could figure is that the wedding was taking place at my church. Could they have just sent out invitations to everyone that happened to be on the church's mailing list? Sheesh, we are talking about a congregation of around 600 to 800 people! Another strange thing was that there was no reply card or any kind of RSVP information. Was it just a whoever-shows-up situation? Not only that, but they committed the usual wedding faux pas by putting where they were registered, which makes it worse this time since apparently they are inviting people whom they don't know! Talk about being desperate for guests!

Guests that you will be inviting to witness your wedding and celebrate at the reception should be close friends and family, not every Tom, Dick, or Mary who has ever had the misfortune to be remotely acquainted with you. You want your invitation to elicit vicarious joy and excitement from your guests, not perplexed confusion as they try to figure out who these people are who are getting married. Sometimes parents, if given unbridled range to the guest list, may be tempted to

The Wedding Consultation

Brideweena: This guest list is getting so long!

Miss Jeanne: Let's review your guest list. Who is on it so far?

Brideweena: Curtis's side of the family totals 133, my family totals 105, our friends are 55, and my coworkers make 20.

Miss Jeanne: Why are you inviting coworkers?

Brideweena: I thought I was supposed to. I mean, I talk with these people every day. Like, you know?

Miss Jeanne: Just because you spend eight hours of every day bonding with other captive humans over your shared Dilbert experiences of cubicle life doesn't mean you are required to invite them to significant social events in your personal life. Do you socialize with these people outside of the office?

Brideweena: Felix the mail-room clerk and I shared a cab once on the way to an employee sensitivity training seminar. Does that count?

Miss Jeanne: I'm afraid not. If you won't even go to a movie with some of these people, why would you invite them to the most important and personal event of your life? Don't get me wrong, you can invite them if the budget allows and your heart dictates, but you are under no obligation to do so. But remember, if you decide not to invite them, it's time to stop blabbing about wedding plans to your officemates.

view the wedding as an opportunity for social pay-backs by inviting coworkers, bosses, old war buddies, and a host of other people you have never laid eyes on in your life. If you think someone might ask, "Brideweena who?" don't invite them.

I know some churches where it has become routine to issue what I refer to as "cattle call" invitations to all church members. These are preprinted invitations on a half sheet of paper that are usually inserted into the Sunday service bulletins as a way to save money on stationery and postage. Everyone and anyone is invited to attend the wedding and the simple reception afterward. The problem with this type of invitation is that too many people treat it with the same regard with which it was issued to them, that is, too casually. Despite being asked to RSVP promptly, many do not, which then requires numerous phone calls to people to find out if they are really attending or not. What you save on postage, you will eat up in time spent calling people. Not having a proper count can matter even with a simple reception since it will affect the amount of cake and punch ordered. With a bigger affair, a surprising number of attendees can be disastrous.

Don't staple your invitation to the company or college bulletin board either.

Rule 2: Are They Guests or Impromptu Caterers?

The invitation to my niece's third wedding stated "Reception at Bride and Groom's Home. Please bring lawn chairs, a side dish, and beverage of choice. We will supply hot dogs and hamburgers." Needless to say, the only thing she will be getting from me is my best wishes. . . .

Give people an invitation directing them to cater your wedding reception and you hand them proof positive of what they may have suspected for years, that you are one tacky little hairball.

While we all want the wedding of our dreams, you can't do it at the expense of others by enlisting them as caterers. Do you really want people there to share in your joy or are they there to share in the catering expenses?

"But, Miss Jeanne, our family has *always* had potluck wedding receptions! It's our cultural heritage."

The problems with that are: (I) It would be presumptuous to assume all your guests are of the same cultural heritage and wouldn't mind being presumed upon to cater the reception, and (2) just because your ancestors may have been rude, cheeky boors you do not have to carry on the family legacy.

Besides, there is a major difference between friends and family volunteering to bring food, versus your assuming people are going to do it when you presumptively assign people food items to bring. I also belong to a cultural group who typically and generously offers to prepare food for weddings. I've done it many times myself. *But*, and it's a big one, at no time can those gifts of food be presumed to be owed and therefore assigned to, commandeered, or directed from the guests.

Rule 3: Know Thy Guests' Guests

This one has probably been told before by hundreds of other people, but this really did hurt my feelings. Let me set the stage first: My fiancé and I got engaged in May of 2002, and we had promptly set our date for May 14, 2003. One of my fiancé's groomsmen, Dean, also got engaged in June of 2002, and he and his fiancée, Anne, set their date for May 7, 2003. They very graciously asked us if this was okay with us, and even postponed their honeymoon by one week so that they could still be in/attend our wedding. Of course, we had no problems with this and were very happy for them.

We are very good friends with Dean and Anne, and we spend lots of time with them, but the primary relationship is between my fiancé and Dean. Our invitations were going out at about the same time as theirs, so I was checking the spelling of her last name to make sure I got it right on my invitations, and I also gave her the correct spelling of my name, assuming she would want it. Two weeks later, we get their invitation in the mail, and the computer-printed label on the invitation was addressed to "Mr. xxxx and guest."

AND GUEST??????????

We go out to dinner often with these people, I gave them the correct spelling of my name, we were engaged before they were, I am going to be my fiancé's wife one week after their wedding, and they were too freaking lazy to put my name on the invitation. It hurts my feelings and basically makes me feel insignificant.

This is, without a doubt, the most frequently expressed offense in regard to invitations. It looks sloppy and lazy on the part of the bridal couple not to have made the effort to extend the invitation to include the significant other of a primary guest by name. Engaged couples certainly do qualify as a soon-to-be single social unit that deserves a properly addressed invitation. Further sloppiness shows up in misspelling names. Come on, your guests are supposed to be dear and beloved friends and family and you can't get the spelling of their names right?

Yet another variation on the importance of "Knowing thy guests' guests" . . .

My college roommate is getting married this June. She is getting married about an hour away from where I live, plus the wedding is at night. So I assumed that she invited me and a guest for that reason.

I replied back to her invitation saying that I was going to bring along my best friend Claire. Now, I was seeing a few people at the same time but I figured instead of bringing a random guy . . . that Claire would be good because the bride knew Claire from when she and I lived together.

I get a call a few days after I assumed the bride-to-be had received my reply to her invite. She said that she assumed I would bring a male with me, and that I would have to disinvite Claire because she was a female! She said that I was "breaking the rules" by bringing "just anyone I wanted" and "everyone knows when you are invited to a wedding that you should bring a significant other."

WHAT??

I would understand if it were a money issue since she is young and probably can't afford to invite many people. But it wasn't that! She even said that I could still bring a guy if I wanted! She had no gripes with Claire at all . . . it was the fact that she wanted a couple wedding! Needless to say, I decided not to go!

If you put "and guest" on your invitations, you have yielded up any say you might have in what other guests your specifically invited guests may bring with them, aside from number ("and guest" means "and *one* guest"). Your guests are free to invite their current paramour, close friend, daughter, or mailman. The bride's problem is that she did not craft an invitation that communicated her desires well. If she intended for significant others to be included as guests, she should have taken the time to find out the names of those significant others and issued the invitations specifically.

The Wedding Consultation

Brideweena: Which computer font do you think would be appropriate for addressing the invitations?

Miss Jeanne: Excuse me, "computer font"?

Brideweena: You know . . . those different styles of writing you can make the computer do? We're addressing the envelopes by printing clear labels and sticking them on the envelope.

Miss Jeanne: Brideweena, what is the impression you want to give people when they receive your invitation?

Brideweena: Elegance! Formality!

Miss Jeanne: Why would you use bulk-mail to announce to your guests this special and, hopefully, once-in-a-lifetime event, your marriage? The ultraspecial events in our lives deserve to be announced to guests with as great a degree of care and personal input as possible.

Brideweena: But my handwriting looks like chicken scratchings, and besides, this is the twenty-first century and using a computer should be commonplace.

Miss Jeanne: That may be so, but slapping a computer label on a wedding-invitation envelope looks lazy and mass produced. You want an announcement to be uniquely expressive of your tastes. When the invitation is hand-addressed, it gives the impression that you took the time personally to write to each guest that his or her presence at your special day is important. Computer-printed mailing labels merely look as if you stacked a bunch of label sheets in the printer tray and hit the print key.

To underscore how guests can perceive computer-printed invitations erroneously, let me tell you of a recent bride who went one step beyond printed labels to actually printing her invitation envelopes by computer. When I received mine, my first impression was that it was a solicitation from a political group inviting hundreds of people to a fund-raising event. I nearly threw it out unopened. I wasn't the only person to perceive it that way. Another guest told me it looked so much like a political fund-raiser invitation that she placed it on her husband's mail pile rather than open it herself.

Brideweena: Okay, okay, I get the idea. I have to accept the fact that my hand is going to be numb from all this handwriting. You are a cruel taskmaster, Miss Jeanne.

Miss Jeanne: Yes, I know. I'm evil personified to the terminally crass. An idea I always suggest to my brides is to host an invitation-addressing dinner. Invite friends who have expressed an interest in helping you with your wedding to a dinner that you prepare, and afterward, divide up the guest list into manageable sections with each friend getting a list, a stack of envelopes, and writing implements. It requires you to be prepared with the proper tools and correct addresses. I did this with my own wedding and it was a very enjoyable evening with plenty of laughter.

Rule 4: What God Has Joined Together, Let No Man Put Asunder

My nephew is getting married in September. Their very traditional invitations came with an enclosed card from The Bay for registry and another card that stated "Sorry, but due to budget constraints, this invitation is only for the person named on the invitation. You will not be able to bring a date or your children to the reception. Thank you for your understanding." The invitation was addressed only to me, not to me and my husband or our children. Everyone else's invitation was addressed this way as well in our family. Only "family" was invited, not the spouses.

When two people marry, they are henceforth to be regarded as a single social unit. When the wedding budget is exceedingly tight, the temptation exists for some people to limit the guest list by excluding spouses. But this is a pennywise and pound foolish choice that is guaranteed to alienate everyone to whom you send this ungracious invitation. People who send out this kind of invitation must have a relational death wish. You might as well put a gun to your address book and pull the trigger because your social life is about to die a hideous death.

It is unnecessary to spell out in crass language that children are not invited to the wedding if you have properly addressed the outer and inner envelopes of the invitation with the names of those in the household that are invited. Yes, I am fully aware that there are guests who will ignore the convention of invitation addressing and insist their children must attend the wedding with them. Some parents have never cut the umbilical cord and any separation from darling little Fufu for more than an hour is unthinkable. Their separation anxiety is not reason for you to put something tacky like "Adult-Only Reception" on the invitation. What kind of reception is this going to be?

Attempts by guests to manipulate you into including the little rugrats with a threat of not attending themselves should be met with firm but polite resistance: "Oh, I'm sorry to hear you won't be attending the wedding. We'll miss you!" There is always a caveat to any rule, and common sense should tell you that nursing mothers of tiny newborns may need an exemption. But don't cave in to Aunt Barbie's insistence that six-year-old Trevor will be permanently scarred for life if he doesn't attend your wedding.

Rule 5: Leave the ABC's Back in Kindergarten Where They Belong

I used to work at a stationery store that specialized in wedding invitations. As you are no doubt aware, invitations traditionally include response cards— those "reply by June 12" cards that guests send back to let the couple know if they'll be at the wedding or not. One couple wondered if it was possible to place two half-orders of response cards with different "reply by" dates on them. The reason? They were planning to send out the invitations in two sets: the "A-list" set would go out first, while the "B-list" set would be sent out after the A-list response deadline had passed, once they knew how much space they had from A-listers who declined the invitation! Second-string wedding guests. Unbelievable.

Peggy Post says you can have A- and B-lists as long as the B-list people don't receive their invitations less than three weeks before the wedding. Peggy Post doesn't read my Etiquette Hell e-mail submissions.

While some argument can be made for prioritizing your guest list, dividing guests into hierarchies of A-, B-, and C-lists is nearly always found out. This always causes offense regardless of how carefully you hide it. To execute A- and B-lists requires some measure of subterfuge and deceit while creatively arranging the timing for mailing of invitations. It's like telling numerous lies and trying to remember whom you told what to so you don't get caught. Invariably guests talk among themselves, and if they are anticipating your invitation, the details will start to emerge as they realize that some of them were on the A-list and others on the B-list.

A girl I worked with at a bank planned her wedding and sent out invitations to the A-list. After the A-list responded, she started to invite a few of us from work.

Really klutzy attempts at segregating guests into hierarchies involve writing *A, B,* or *C* lightly penciled in on a corner of the invitation or sending an invitation either shortly before the wedding date or after the RSVP deadline has passed. Such obtuse behavior clues guests in that they did not make the A-list and are second-thought guests. I received a B-list invitation once. I was surprised because our social interaction seemed to indicate we were closer than the reality the invitation uncovered. Upon further discussion with A-list guests, it became apparent that the couple had chosen a very expensive reception venue, requiring them to limit their guest list to be able to afford it. It was with dawning shock that I realized the price of a prime rib dinner was more precious to the engaged couple than my presence at their wedding, so I readjusted the parameters of my social circle to reflect this new reality of the relationship.

Compose your list of whom you desire to be at your wedding and then select the venue that can accommodate the number of people you wish to invite. Adjust your budget to accommodate that number as well. It is far better to serve cake and punch in the warm glow of all one's friends than dine on caviar and stoke the glowing coals of enmity in former friends. Those who come will come. Adding people at the last minute to fill in for those who decline the initial invitations gives the appearance of desperation as well as simply inviting warm bodies who just might also bring a nice wedding present.

Rule 6: Innies and Outies

We received a wedding invitation from my fiancé's cousin. So many things about it were wrong. The outer envelope had my fiancé's name and address on it, and there was no inner envelope, so we were unsure whether I and our son were even invited. (We'd been living together for eight years by this point.) My fiancé had to call and see if I was invited, and whether children were allowed, which we were, so I'm not sure why they didn't put it on the envelope!

To save money on postage, some people forgo the inner envelope to decrease the weight. There is nothing wrong in doing this, but if you do not address the outer envelope with the names of all those invited to the wedding, you can expect confusion from guests. Believe it or not, there are actually real people in this world who do understand the etiquette of invitations, and if you don't use the standard method of informing people who in the household is actually invited, you can expect to spend precious time fielding phone calls. Or worse, people will view it as an open invitation to bring whomever they want.

Rule 7: RSVPPPPPPP

To top it all off, there was no stamp on the return envelope, so we either had to pay for a stamp, or make a long-distance phone call to reply . . . which is fine for us, but really tacky on their part.

Traditional etiquette does not even require you to put an RSVP card and envelope in the invitation at all, since the obligation traditionally fell to the guests to break out pen and paper to express their intent to attend the wedding or not. But sometimes changes in the prevailing culture demand a resultant change in etiquette, and while it is technically acceptable not to include an RSVP reply card, many guests will be at a loss as to how to respond because they have come to expect one. Given how poor the response rate can be even with a reply card, it's best to not challenge the guests to climb even the tiniest of hurdles to respond. As for the lack of postage stamp on the RSVP return envelope, over time this has come to be perceived by guests as cheap and an unnecessary inconvenience to them. While it may seem unfair that you get saddled with this added postage expense, not to provide it runs the risk of guests just not bothering to reply.

Rule 8: Presentation Hesitation Is a Good Thing

The invite itself was okay, professionally printed, but there were some words at the bottom, near the reception information, that we didn't understand. Next to the hotel address, it said "Presentation Preferred." We thought this perhaps meant that we had to bring the invite to the hotel, to prove that we were guests or something. When my fiancé called, he asked what this meant. . . . His cousin hemmed and hawed for a bit, but managed to explain that this meant they didn't want gifts, but preferred to be presented with money. Since these invites were not homemade, that means some stationery specialist somewhere neglected to inform them how tacky this was . . . or the happy couple ignored the advice.

I admit to being completely baffled by "Presentation Preferred" on a wedding invitation when I first encountered it. It looks so formal that it deceives you into thinking at first that it must be proper etiquette. After all, the engraver put it on the invitation and engravers know proper etiquette, don't they? I made several inquiries to those whose opinion I respect and discovered the meaning of "Presentation Preferred." Translation: I'm a greedy little sucker; give me money.

The inclusion of "Presentation Preferred" on a wedding invitation is a heinous scheme invented by some greedy, sneaky money-grubber who devised a way to inform guests of her avarice while clothing it in formal language implying that it is proper etiquette. Such highbrow wording gives the impression that this is a more socially suitable method of begging for money than boorishly obvious pleas for cash. In extreme examples of presentation, guests line up at the reception literally to present their monetary gifts to the newlyweds, evoking mental images of the subdued tribes of Africa paying homage to Pharaoh on his throne.

A variant of the "Presentation Preferred" invitation is one in which the request for cash is far more blatant. It includes notification of impending reception activities such as money trees, money dances, or other ingenious games meant to separate guests from their cash.

As the lifestyles editor for a local newspaper, I have the pleasure of editing the engagement and wedding announcements submitted to the paper.

The most memorable was the darling bride-to-be who wanted to include in her published engagement announcement the following information: "A money dance will be held at the reception. Food stamps will be accepted."

Needless to say, I used my "editorial judgment" to exclude that tidbit.

Then there's the more direct approach:

I received an invitation in the mail for a former coworker's wedding. The invitation contained a blank deposit form for a bank account bearing the names of the bride and the groom.

Invitations that solicit monetary donations of any type cause Miss Jeanne to develop a severe case of "ornery guest syndrome" which compels me to do exactly the opposite of what the invitation suggests. A suitably ornery gift from a justifiably ornery guest would be some ubiquitous countertop appliance such as a cheap can opener, or, in more heightened states of orneriness, a gift basket consisting entirely of money-related gag gifts such as chocolate coins or candy money.

The Wedding Consultation

Brideweena: What does this "M_____" line on the RSVP reply card mean?

Miss Jeanne: I'm not sure what the origin of that is but the idea is to write "Mr. and Mrs. Joe Schmoo will or will not attend" on that line. Please tell me you haven't added "Number of Guests Attending" on the RSVP too?

Brideweena: Uh, yes, I was thinking of that because I need to know how many people are coming.

Miss Jeanne: You might want to reconsider putting that on the reply card. I can't tell you how many times I've heard of guests who view this as open season for inviting as many extra guests as they like. While you may have issued the invitation to a friend and her husband, they may add on several children, adult friends, and a few pets. If you do this, be prepared to receive responses with more people than you invited, and you will then need to make awkward phone calls to correct.

Brideweena: Why would anyone want to bring their pet to a wedding?

Miss Jeanne: Considering the behavior of some children, a pet dog might be a vast improvement on the quality of guests.

Rule 9: Accept the Declinations with Grace

I met Joy five years ago when we were on a committee together. We were pretty friendly for a while but then she started dating John, who was also on the committee, so she didn't have time to socialize with me. Around a year later she and John got engaged. She invited me to her wedding, which was two years ago. It was a Saturday-evening, black-tie affair and I was invited solo, without a date (at the time I had been dating my boyfriend for a few months). I was unable to attend because I had a family party the same night.

When I sent back my response, "Regretfully unable to attend," I received a voice-mail message from her. She said, "I just got your response and I can't believe that you are not coming to my wedding. I know it is because I invited you without your boyfriend. We only invited people's boyfriend/girlfriend if they have been dating for more than a year. There is a singles table that we are going to seat you at. Please call me immediately." I called her back and got her answering machine so I left her a message and told her that I was unable to attend because I had a family party the same evening and was sorry I would miss her wedding. I told her that she should call me back if she wanted to talk further about it. I never heard from her.

Even though I was unable to attend her wedding, of course I wanted to send her a wedding gift so I went to a nice shop, bought her a beautiful bowl, and had it shipped to her home. Around two months later I received a note that said:

Dear Alexis,

We received the gift you sent. I still can't believe that you did not come to my wedding. I miss our friendship, but things can never be the same.

I wish you the best.

Needless to say that is the rudest, tackiest, and most classless note I have ever received.

I don't know whether I can top the writer's list of adjectives used to describe this bride's note. While a wedding is a momentous event in the lives of those involved, to others it is just another blip on the social calendar. Alexis honored her obligation to a previously committed event but this wasn't good enough for the self-centered bride who couldn't fathom why anyone would decline an invitation to her fabulous wedding.

Immutable Fact of Life

Mrs. Frito Jones and the late Mr. Frito Jones request the honour of your presence at the marriage of their daughter . . .

If you put the name of a deceased parent on the invitation as a co-host, expect to creep out your guests. Dead people cannot host social events or issue invitations.

Rule 10: Always Advance, Never Retreat

Quite a few years back, a close girlfriend of mine got engaged to her longtime boyfriend. I was in a serious relationship at the time and we were both invited (by name, not "guest") to their engagement party, which was elaborate enough to rival most weddings I've ever been to. Months later, I also attended her bridal shower and was actually seated with some of her bridesmaids (all relatives) as a "guest of honor." My boyfriend and I received the wedding invitation the same week and it was addressed to both of us (but sent to my address). We shopped for a gift together and ended up getting them a gift certificate to one of the places where they registered because most of the stuff on the registry had already been bought. Six days before the wedding, my friend calls me and says that she has had a lot of relatives respond unexpectedly—at the last minute— that they are coming, and they had to cut back the number of guests. She asked that I come as a single and not bring my boyfriend of three years! I was so totally bummed that I made up an excuse not to attend the wedding though I did send the gift certificate we had purchased.

A tight budget is no excuse for the social cloddishness of retracting an invitation once issued. This is such a commonsense etiquette rule that one wonders whether people are truly as socially inept as their behavior would imply. It is not uncommon for people to invite more guests than the venue can accommodate in the belief that some undetermined percentage of them will decline the invitation and not attend, thus giving them the exact number of guests they want. However, this can backfire when fewer guests decline than was expected. If you find yourself in this situation, just suck it up and deal with it. Retracting an invitation is a very serious faux pas. No amount of Clorox will wash away that "Tacky" label people will mentally brand you with if you are stupid enough actually to retract an invitation once issued.

Rule 11: Wedding Announcements Are Not Pleas for Booty

I received the following wedding announcement a full year after the couple in question had tied the knot. Moreover, the announcement was addressed only to me, though the couple is much better friends with my husband.

Claudia and Trevor Smith
happily announce
the recent marriage

of their daughter
Muffin Louise Smith
to
Jim-Bob Jones
son of
Jane and William Jones.
Should you choose to honor their union,
in lieu of a gift,
contributions to the home purchasing fund
would be appreciated.

We sent them a picture frame, and of course we never received a thank-you note. I should say, however, that this plea for cash has provided us with a great dinner-party show-and-tell.

No one was fooled by the very belated, and very obvious, solicitation for money disguised as a benevolent wedding announcement. "Hey, you! Not only were you not good enough to attend my daughter's wedding, but I couldn't have been bothered to inform you of her marriage in a timely fashion. But maybe you might be enough of a foolish sucker, uh, . . . um, beloved friend, to contribute some cash to their mortgage fund as a wedding gift."

I'm always amazed at the sheer audacity of people who try to perpetrate these schemes on people. They have to have a presumption that there are enough gullible boobs in the world willing to send money to make their effort worthwhile. If you have been the recipient of such an invitation or announcement, consider yourself very fortunate that you have discovered your friends' true low opinion of you earlier in the relationship rather than later.

If you intend to send out marriage announcements, the etiquette is to send them very shortly after the wedding, say, within a month at most. Inclusion of registry information is strictly forbidden.

Rule 12: Don't Send That Save-the-Date Card and Not Invite Them

I lived and worked in a small college town and befriended one of the students there, I'll call her Sabrina. When I moved away for another job we kept in touch through phone calls and e-mails. After graduating from college she met her future husband at her first job. They decided to marry in the autumn of 2001 and although I was not living in the same town we spoke of the upcoming event, and I was verbally told to "hold the date" for her wedding.

As the date of the wedding drew near I waited for the invitation to arrive. When it got to be only a few weeks before the wedding, and still no invitation, I figured this was a small wedding and as I was not living near her she decided not to invite me; however, I did want to acknowledge her marriage, so I sent a card and check. The check, I noticed, was cashed ASAP yet I never received a thank-you—not verbal, nor through e-mail, nor written. It seems a bit weird to make a point of telling someone your wedding date and then not inviting them.

In the first flush of just-engaged excitement, resist the urge to stand on the rooftops and announce to the entire world that they need to mark their calendars for your wedding extravaganza. People will take you at your word and will expect eventually to see a wedding invitation grace their mailboxes.

The next step up in formality from a verbal "save the date" is an e-mailed one:

I understand that save-the-date e-mails, so common with Gen Xers these days, are not guarantees of a forthcoming invitation to the actual wedding, but I think more young people need to think before sending them. In the past year, DH and I have received two such e-mails from old friends that specifically told us to mark the date for their weddings. We did, reserving those weekends when we might have made other plans, since six to eight weeks can be short notice in the summer months.

We never received invites from either couple. In fact, all contact stopped between these couples and us around the time that invites were sent, and then miraculously the contact began again a few months after the wedding. Why would I want to resume a friendship with someone who so obviously found me not worthy of attending their wedding?

"Save the date" notices are sent only to those people whom you intend to invite to the wedding. If you give any hint to people that they should designate a specific date as the sacred wedding date on their calendars, then you had better make sure you invite them to the wedding. The rudeness of not following through with an invitation cannot be underestimated. People's lives are not yours to command. Jerking them to and fro with promises of invitations subsequently withheld is cruel and foolish.

Brideweena's Checklist

1. Have I allowed myself plenty of time to choose an invitation style and get it ordered?

2. Have I ordered extra invitations?

3. Do I have my organizational system arranged to keep track of responses?

4. Have I checked postage for the invitations after I have stuffed them?

5. Did I make sure all my guests' names are correctly spelled?

6. Did I make sure to include all significant others by name on invitations?

7. Are all invitation inserts such as maps and hotel directions prepared?

8. Did I remember to tell the department store registry assistant to take a flying leap into Etiquette Hell for daring to suggest it was okay to put the store's registry cards in the invitation?

9. Does the paper weight and font style reflect the tone of my wedding?

10. Is the font style consistent on all my ordered stationery?

Has It Registered Yet?

The excellence of a gift lies in its appropriateness rather than in its value. —CHARLES DUDLEY WARNER

THE HISTORY OF REGISTRIES began somewhat innocuously about a hundred years ago when department stores offered to record a bride's silver and china patterns so guests could buy the right item. But wedding vendors can rarely be trusted to follow the rules of etiquette when the acquisition of a dollar is at stake. Registries became a great way to bring business into the retail establishment at which the bride had registered. Who cared if the Etiquette Mavens of Yore were having apoplectic fits over their tea and crumpets at the scandalous concept that brides would dare to presume to tell their guests what to give them? Registries were viewed as a necessary evil as long as certain rules of decorum and restraint were employed by the bride.

However, what started out as a restrained list of colors and patterns has metastasized into a gimme gift orgy. An engaged couple can register at home building supply stores, mortgage loan companies, travel agencies, banks, sporting goods stores, car dealerships, electronics stores, appliance stores. Wedding vendors are now even offering "registries" so that guests can choose to give a "gift" toward paying for their very expensive wedding services. These businesses will all whisper sweet assurances that it is certainly permissible to include their registry cards in the wedding invitations or place the registry Web site address on every wedding-related piece of paper. What do they care if you end up looking like an etiquette-challenged greedball? I'm convinced that the registry is the sole reason some people enter into the matrimonial state. You can put up with a pretty ugly spouse if you know there are thousands of dollars in prizes awaiting your entry into marital bliss.

Rule 1: Greed—It's an Ugly Thing

We all belonged to the same church and were basically middle-class people. When we went to consult the engaged couple's bridal registry at a big department store, we were shocked to find that they registered for the most expensive item in each category.

We couldn't even afford half a place setting... which was about $250/place setting. We opted to buy the towels they registered for and had to go in with two other people to afford them—on sale.

I later heard their family ended up buying the china set they wanted and that hardly anyone bought gifts from the registry. The wedding was dubbed the "Soak the Friends" party. Everyone was so riled.

Nearly all stores now have scanner "guns" which allow you and your beloved to rampage through the store like kids in a toy store to create a registry wish list. Point the scanner gun at the Universal

Product Code and *poof!* It's instantly entered into the computerized system for your registry. With such ease of registering, it's not hard to go completely insane with greed. Go bonkers shooting the registry scanner gun and your guests may wish they could shoot you for conspicuous consumption and greed. You need to provide a balanced list of registry items that cover a wide range of prices. Remember what my husband says: moderation in everything, including moderation.

Rule 2: Taking Registries to a New Low in Greed

My husband and I are at that point in life when many of our friends are getting married. We are very happy for them and are always happy to attend the weddings if possible and at the least to send a thoughtful gift. We were delighted that so many friends could attend our wedding a year ago and want everyone to have an equally pleasant experience. However, I was utterly shocked when I recently saw the following registry page on a friend's wedding Web site. We, along with all the other guests, received save-the-date cards directing us to the site for further information. The site itself was lovely, except for the following page. Please keep in mind as well that the wedding is in Europe and most of our friends live in the U.S. As we are all relatively recent college graduates and starting out in life, attending the wedding itself will be a huge expense that few of us expect to afford.

"We have registered at several places. We prefer the honeymoon registry over others. Gifts may be mailed to our United States address: [address omitted]. Purchase part of the honeymoon to Hawaii: We will be staying at the Aloha Resort for eight nights. There, we will be sailing, diving, and enjoying the sun and beach. Sponsor miles: Two plane tickets with total mileage of 13,400 miles (23 cents a mile). Sponsor lodging: One full day/night ($150 per day). Sponsor meals: Breakfast ($15 each) Lunch ($19 each) Dinner ($35 each). Sponsor cocktails: Nonalcoholic ($4 each) Alcoholic ($8 each). Sponsor taxi transfers: ($5 to $60 each). Sponsor bike hire: Each ($10 per day). Sponsor car hire: One day ($85). Sponsor a snorkel outing: Each ($18 per half hour). Sponsor a scuba outing: Day ($60 per two-tank dive) Night ($72 per one-tank dive). Sponsor an afternoon sail: Each ($20 per half hour). Sponsor a massage: Each ($40 per half hour). Sponsor a tour of the island: Each ($100). Sponsor a beach picnic: Each ($25). Sponsor a watersports lesson: Each ($15 per half hour)."

There is something quietly sinister about a wedding registry that appears either to increase the happy couple's investment portfolio or expand their traveling opportunities. Are people marrying for love and commitment or is the objective to obtain money, real estate, or the perfect vacation via a trip to the altar?

But all is not rosy even with a honeymoon or mortgage registry. Nearly all such registries charge a fee for the registry or a percentage of the total amount received. "Thank you for your gift, Aunt Fifi! It went to pay for the registry service fee." Some registries that receive cash from guests toward the honeymoon will not refund the unused balance in cash but will only credit it toward your next vacation. Guests are beginning to get savvy about these registries and are refusing to fund some business's profit margin.

Rule 3: Don't Shove It in Their Faces

An acquaintance of mine invited me to her wedding, as well as two of her many showers. On both shower invites, it mentioned where she was registered, and that is fine by me. Shower invitations usually mention a registry. But when I received the actual wedding invitation, registry cards were enclosed! I always thought that inviting people to your wedding was about sharing your special day, not getting as many presents as possible!

The Wedding Consultation

Brideweena: How *does* one inform her guests of a registry? I didn't even want to register because I think it's like begging for gifts. My fiancé Curtis insists that it is just a nice way of letting people know what they could get, so we won't have to return an unwanted gift. A woman I know who was a wedding planner said that she usually put registry information on a sheet that had a map of the wedding location and put this sheet in the invitations. But I read on your site that it is extremely tacky to put any mention of a registry anywhere near an invitation.

Miss Jeanne: Registry information is not supposed to be "push" information where guests are inundated with unsolicited hints as to where you are registered. If guests want to know where you are registered, they will "pull" that information from your mother or a bridesmaid. Amazingly enough, people know whom to call to get that information if they want it.

And by the way, that doesn't mean you can sneak the registry in the back door by putting its Web site address on the map to the wedding sent with the invitation.

Some wedding registry attendants in department stores will hand you a stack of these little cards with the store name on them and slyly lead you into evil. They will whisper lies about how putting these into every invitation is not only acceptable but actually a kindness to your guests who have had their brains sucked from them and need assistance in knowing exactly what you want. Resist the urge to scatter your registry cards among the fertile fields of friends and family, hoping for an even bigger "crop" of gifts.

Rule 4: Don't Spam the Poor People

I lost touch with a college roommate on purpose because she only contacted me when she needed something. I hadn't spoken to her in five years when one day I received an e-mail from her—she had found me on a high school alumni Web site. In her e-mail she informed me that she was getting married. I wrote her back with congratulations, mentioned that I had been married just a few months before, asked her some questions, and so on. Well, she never replied to my e-mail, and I soon forgot about the whole thing. However, during the last few weeks I've begun receiving e-mailed notices from different stores informing me that this friend has registered with them. I've received about six now—it appears she is supplying them with my e-mail address in hopes that I will send her a gift. Her wedding is only a month away according to her original e-mail, and I never received an invitation. I assume I have not been invited to attend but have only been invited to buy her a present!

Don't abuse people and put their names, postal addresses, or e-mail addresses on any piece of literature associated with a wedding vendor. That some vendors are willing to spam your friends and family to kingdom come or deluge them with junk mail should be a powerful indicator that they have no particular concerns for your reputation.

Rule 5: Registries Are Only a Suggestion, Not a Mandate

The usual silly bridal shower games were played and then it was time for the presents. The bride had her older sister, who was matron of honor, sitting on one side with a pad of paper to write down who gave what, and her younger sister, who was a bridesmaid, on her other side with a printed-out copy of the bride and groom's registry! As the gifts were opened the bride exclaimed happily when the gift came from the registry, and her sister smiled and crossed the item off the list. Whenever a present wasn't from the registry the bride promptly put it down and either opened the box, or searched the gift bag for the receipt! If she didn't find one she'd ask the person who had given her the present if she had kept a copy! She explained that since she wanted everything in her new home to match, anything that wasn't from the registry and that didn't match her predetermined decor would be sent back and the cash obtained put toward the honeymoon!

Now, I understand many couples return wedding gifts that are either duplicates or just not anything they feel they can reasonably use, but to tell the giver to her face that her gift was not wanted? She even had the nonregistry gifts placed in the back corner of the room where the shower was being held, and at the end of the event had her picture taken only with the pile of gifts that were from her registry!

And to top it all off, since many of us invited to the shower were also going to be attending the wedding/reception to be held in three weeks, she had copies of the updated registry given to those who had given her the nonregistry gifts! Tacky tacky tacky!

Etiquette Mavens recoiled in horror at the concept of wedding registry because it had the potential for the bride to presume that gifts were expected and that guests could be directed what to give. Of course, well-mannered, gracious brides wouldn't dream of being so rude as to tell someone her gift is below par because it wasn't from the registry. Just because you register for potential gifts, doesn't mean your guests are obligated to buy from your registry.

I've given orders to my battalions of Ornery Guests that should they encounter such a situation as related above, they are apologetically to assume possession of the noxious gift with offers to take it back. What the unsuspecting bride doesn't know is that Ornery Guests will return the gift for a refund that they may either spend on an etiquette book for the bride or keep the cash for themselves.

Rule 6: Registries Are Not for Money Laundering

I work nights and weekends for a national department store, which is probably the most popular store in the country for registering for weddings. I am getting married in a few months myself (we are paying for it ourselves which is why I am working there as a second job), and I am appalled at the behavior of some of the couples that come in before and after their weddings. I work in the china and crystal department, which is also the bridal registry department, so I deal with these couples daily. My department is unique in that we generally develop relationships with many of our customers, whether they are wedding guests or the wedding couple. I have also created a registry for myself at the store, mainly after being badgered by friends and family.

Every week I have couples who register for items they do not want or need, with the express intention of returning them for what they really want afterward (be it furniture, china, etc.). Every week I have couples returning these items for store credit, or to their store credit card to reduce their balance. We also have a lot of people who become upset that we do not provide cash refunds for anything, unless it was paid for in cash and they have the receipt.

I see registry lists that are six feet long when printed out (no joke), and customers who are confused as to what they are obligated to purchase. I gently try to let customers know that they are not actually obligated to purchase anything, let alone purchase four or five gifts for the various parties and showers. Most customers are happy to hear this, and many make comments about "gift grabs." The store I work at is located smack-dab in the most affluent area in my state, and we hear about a lot of couples who have engagement parties and several showers. While tacky, it is not terribly uncommon in this area. I hear lots of couples talking about how much "loot" they're going to acquire while picking things for their registry.

I do not just deal with greedy couples—I also deal with wonderful brides and grooms, guests, and family members. I have had the pleasure of serving an elderly grandmother who bought every single piece of china on the registry, so that she would know her granddaughter would have it if she passed away before the wedding. (I had a hard time not crying while I helped her.) I have helped sisters and mothers and best friends and brothers who are so happy about the upcoming nuptials that they have cried while picking things out. Some of these couples and guests have also given me great ideas for my own wedding, and I have had a good time talking about their plans with them.

Anyway, on to my main point. Last week, I had a woman come in to start a registry (twenty minutes prior to closing). She was asking numerous questions, such as how do items get returned, what kind of credit do you get for returning things, etc. This was obviously a case of another bride planning to return her gifts. She wanted to know if the returns could be credited to a store *credit card, to which I said yes. She then asked if she opened an account, re- turned all of the gifts, and then closed the card, how would the credit balance be returned to her? I advised that she would need to speak to the credit department about that, but that it would either be issued as a store credit or a check. She in- sisted I call them immediately to find out. (This was right as the store was closing.) I managed to get hold of someone in credit before they closed for the evening, and found out that it would be returned as a check. This seemed to please her, and she let on that all of the other stores she had checked would have issued store credit (which is why she chose not to register at them). I guess that was the deciding factor in her choosing my store to register at. She kept myself and another girl there for an hour after the store closed, picking items for her registry, and yes, applying for a store credit card. She also kept asking me about the gifts I have received for my upcoming wedding. (She assumed I was getting married after noticing my ring.) She wanted to know how much money people were spending on us, and if I was getting gifts I registered for. (The answer is yes, and I have truly appreciated each gift and have written and sent the thank- you cards the same day I have received them.) She seemed shocked to hear that I was actually keeping the gifts I have received instead of returning them. Al- though she was mostly polite and friendly, I couldn't help but think how tacky this is. I'm sure I'll be seeing her again soon, when she returns all of her gifts and closes the account.*

Pay attention: this is one of the rare wedding-registry attendants who actually knows her etiquette and has the right perspective.

Registries have become convenient money-laundering schemes in which couples register for outrageously expensive gifts or items they would never really want for the sole purpose of returning the item for cash or store credit. Stores have now caught on to this and have begun being more restrictive in their policies. It's a sneaky way to get the cash you really want for the wedding under the guise of registering. Poor schmuck guests actually believe the charade and carefully choose gifts from the registry under the delusion that you really want the items for which you registered. But it's all a game, a little con game at the expense of the department store and your guests. With abuses of registries like this, is it any wonder guests are becoming increasingly leery of even glancing at the registry?

Brideweena's Checklist

1. Have I registered where most of my guests can easily access the registry list?

2. Have I constrained my greed and registered for what I need?

3. Have I plastered I WILL BE GRATEFUL signs all over the bathroom mirror and my computer monitor in the event I receive gifts not on my registry?

4. Have I sworn to gnaw my trigger finger to the bone before I will register for M&M's, underwear, or an X-Box for the kids?

5. Did I give the printer the evil eye for daring to suggest putting the registry information on the invitations?

FIVE

Shower Thy Love

A gift —be it a present, a kind word, or a job done with care and love—explains itself!...and if receivin' it embarrasses you, it's because your "thanks box" is warped. —ALICE CHILDRESS

*J*JUST LOVE SHOWERS—REALLY, I DO. In its purest form, a shower is a celebration of friends and family joyfully bestowing blessings on appreciative brides. In less pure form, though, the shower degrades quickly into a gift-grubbing bonanza on a par with winning the showcase showdown on *The Price Is Right*.

The nature of a shower is that people are invited with the expectation that they are bringing wedding-related gifts to "shower" the guest of honor in preparation for her entry into married life. Showers are a test of our character that exposes our true nature of either gratitude or greed. If they venture onto the slippery slope of avarice, brides and their mothers and sisters are all tempted to devise creative ways to obtain the choicest booty with the presumption that the bride deserves all she can get.

Rule 1: Those Who Attend the Showers, Attend the Wedding

A good friend of mine that I hadn't seen in a while was to be married to a great guy. I received my shower invitation as did a mutual friend and we went to the shower together.

During the drive over we discussed if we were invited to the wedding, or reception. The shower was lovely, as was the food. I was acquainted with a couple of the women at the shower, and we discussed the wedding plans. We enjoyed watching the bride unwrap the gifts. I took great care in selecting a beautiful negligee in her favorite color. She loved it. All the while she talked about the wedding, and who was in the wedding party, who was invited. As it turned out, driving partner and I weren't invited! Seems this was just a big wedding with people who are "important" in our industry, and since she and I really don't have any clout in their eyes, we didn't rate an invitation.

This is one etiquette rule brides are willing to flout because they deceive themselves into believing that their shower guests really do want to share the bride's "joy" even if they cannot attend the wedding. Being used as a means to increase someone else's material assets is not very high on my personal list of enjoyable life experiences. There is nothing worse than finding out you are not invited to the wedding while in the midst of attending a shower. Your presence at the wedding isn't wanted but your gifts sure are! There is no way to sugarcoat this faux pas to make it acceptable. Do it and you can guarantee a drastic change in your relationships with those shower guests who don't qualify for a wedding invitation.

As the bride, you have an obligation to give the shower hostess an accurate list of whom to invite and that list should be limited solely to your invited wedding guests.

Rule 2: Shower Me Not with Avon

I was recently invited to a bridal shower for a friend—via e-mail. In the e-mail, the time and place were announced, and the process for gifts was described. The bride's sister sells Tupperware products, and the catalog would be available for the guests to make their purchases at the shower! I didn't go, simply because it was so gauche.

Isn't that sweet? They are trying to make it as convenient as possible for the guests to buy gifts while padding their own little pockets to boot.

I received the invitation, and I almost fell over backward when I read it! The bride's twin sister, who was also the maid of honor, was hosting the shower, but it wasn't a "regular" bridal shower. What it was, was a "party" featuring a line of adult toys, creams, lotions, with a sexual orientation. The invitation specified that we'd be "given the opportunity" to purchase selected items for the bride and groom. (Eeeew!) It also read, "please bring a friend and receive a special gift!" A good-natured work friend of mine expressed interest in attending with me, so I decided, sure, why not, I'll bite. I think it's extremely tacky to sell a product line to a captive audience, but I didn't want to hurt the bride's feelings, which would have been even tackier. We sat and drank beer and listened to the spiel, but the demonstrator took so long helping each guest with their purchases that I didn't get a chance to purchase any of her products. (Oh, darn!) Instead of any of these tacky products, I gave the bride a beautiful lingerie set. To this day, I laugh and scratch my head when I think back on the tackiness of it all.

Sometimes brides are in on this and sometimes they are not. In both situations, a sister is taking advantage of a captive audience to hit the sales quota for her business. The guests are being used as pawns to financially benefit the host under the guise of being "helpful." Often the bride is just as much a victim since she may not have had a clue that this was to be perpetrated on the shower guests. The host becomes the parasite leeching off the marketing opportunities a wedding can offer. A captive audience is primed to buy gifts for the bride, so they are ripe for the picking by a con artist who is all too happy to ride the wedding gravy train.

Rule 3: Showers Are Not Fund-Raising Events

A coworker was telling me all about the Jack and Jill party he had attended on the weekend. A Jack and Jill is, apparently, a shared male/female sort of party that is held a few weeks prewedding. This particular Jack and Jill was to include the following tasteful elements:

- *An admission price. Tickets were $10 per person.*
- *A cash bar, manned by the wedding party, the profits of which would go toward the expenses of the wedding.*
- *A raffle that the guests could buy tickets on. (The prize, I later found out, was one of the wedding gifts that had been sent early.)*
- *Some casino-style games, in which the players gambled with real money but all the winnings went to the happy couple.*

At first, I hadn't been paying that much attention to the details, but throughout this whole terrible recitation, my level of horror was increasing. When my coworker stopped telling me about it, I declared it to be sort of tacky-sounding. Imagine, using your friends to pay for your wedding that way.

A "Jack and Jill" can be a name for a dual-gender or couples' shower. Unfortunately, it can also refer to a fund-raising party hosted either by the bridal attendants or by the Happy Couple themselves in order to raise enough cash to afford a wedding beyond their means. The primary objective is to extract the maximum amount of cash from every warm, breathing body there under the guise of gambling or games in which the only winner is the bride and groom. I've heard every excuse imaginable for the existence of this type of fund-raiser, the most common being that it's an artifact of the couple's cultural identity. This, of course, offends the living bejeebers out of their fellow countrymen, who wouldn't inflict this on the local rat population, let alone anyone they know, and are offended that they've been lumped into this stereotype by their peers.

Jack and Jills are not a Canadian thing. They are not an Australian thing. They aren't any kind of cultural "thing" other than a greedy, use-your-friends-and-acquaintances-as-cash-machines kind of thing. If your friends think they are a great idea, it's only because they are greedy little monsters only too happy to suck the cash from people when their matrimonial turn comes. If you can't afford the wedding of your dreams, scale back your plans or wait a while and save up. Don't siphon the difference out of your friends' wallets.

Rule 4: Show Some Respect, Some Inkling of Emotions, Anything

My cousin was sitting on a platform in a chair surrounded by the wedding party and the presents. She was handed a present, opened it, held it up, and then passed it off to an attendant. Never once did she say who the gift was from, that she liked it, etc. Nothing. Not even an ooohhh or ahhhhh. Just open the loot, pass it on, and grab the next gift. While this show was going on, the chil-

dren that came to the shower were right in front of the stage running, yelling, screaming. Suddenly, a few of the kids ran up on the stage and started grabbing presents and ripping them open. Everyone, including the mothers, the bride, and her attendants were giggling at how "cute" the kids were, and no one was even attempting to stop them from ripping open packages. That went on for about half an hour. Then I saw one of my presents being opened and broken by one of the children. I was so disgusted, I quietly said my good-byes to the ladies at my table and left without being obvious. I could not believe I drove six hours to attend this bridal shower. It was a disgusting attempt for the bridal party to procure gifts from everyone the bride had invited to the wedding disguised as a scene from Animal House.

It's pretty bad when the bride is the greedy savage devouring her gifts with nary a grunt of gratitude between "mouthfuls," but to unleash the tiny barbarians on the gifts was truly an act of total disdain for the guests' efforts at shopping for the perfect gift and carefully wrapping it.

You need to set the example of decorum, grace, and patience for the knee nibblers. Little girls nearly worship a bride and can be very much influenced by your behavior. You wouldn't want it to be known that your lapses in graciousness inspired the next generation of Bridezillas in your community, would you?

Immutable Fact of Life

People will perceive you as an ungrateful little wretch if you can't find the strength to muster a smidgen of comment about the gift they have brought you. When actor Roberto Benigni won an unexpected Academy Award for best actor, his reaction was to jump out of his chair, kiss his wife and *Life Is Beautiful* costar Nicoletta Braschi, then run up and down the aisle, hugging people and shaking hands. When asked later about his actions, he stated, "It's a sign of mediocrity when you demonstrate gratitude with moderation." He's right. Act like a dead bump on a log and people will presume you couldn't care less about what you are receiving.

Rule 5: The Shower Registry Is Not an Ultimatum

Last year, my coworker Sylvia was engaged, and made a few faux pas (faux passes?). The first was at her bridal shower. One of the guests, Tina, who is the absolute epitome of good manners and class, had purchased a lovely set of pots and pans as a gift. Tina's present was the first one opened, whereupon Sylvia loudly exclaimed, "Who the hell bought this? I don't cook!" She had forgotten that her fiancé had put it on their "wish list" at the registry, and Sylvia thought the shower gift was a joke. Tina, of course, was mortified.

Must . . . control . . . Ornery . . . Guest . . . Syndrome! How might one confront such a rude, ungracious, evil bride? Perhaps by feigning embarrassment at having offended her delicate sensibilities in selecting the incorrect gift. You could then take possession of it to return it for something more appropriate to the needs of the recipient . . . such as a pretty little muzzle.

Ingratitude, though, is not solely the domain of those whose tongues are disconnected from their brains. You can offend people with less dramatic displays of ingratitude.

I was one of the unfortunate ones who hadn't bought her a gift from her registry, but since my gift was a rather large collection of basic house-cleaning supplies (Windex, 409, Pine-Sol, sponges, rubber gloves) I got off relatively easy with only a grimace and the comment "Oh . . . what an interesting gift." I did not "rekindle" the friendship, and I'm sure the bride lost many more friends that day.

It's a fact that you will receive gifts that you did not register for, gifts you will utterly despise and have no interest in keeping whatsoever. Guests will try to buy you what they think you will like. But, let's face it, some people won't know your tastes all that well or they will be limited by their budget. You will end up with Precious Moments coffee mugs and lingerie only the Amish would find alluring.

Think of your shower as a time when you are on stage with people watching closely to see whether you like the gifts they have given you. They will gauge every nuance of your facial expressions to discern your delight upon opening the present. Women, in particular, love to watch each other open gifts as a sort of female-bonding thing. Grimacing is not allowed. Disinterest is discouraged. Yawning is verboten. Audible gasps of horror are to be squelched. Gag reflexes should be reined in. Use of the word "interesting" to describe a gift is code for being so stunned over someone buying you such an atrocious gift that you can only choke out the lame epithet "interesting." Say instead "unique." Say "precious." Say "thoughtful." Say "arresting." Say any of a thousand things; just don't say "interesting."

The Wedding Consultation

Brideweena: I just know Aunt Fifi will give me a complete set of crocheted toilet-paper-roll covers shaped like Barbie dolls on steroids. I can't fake that I just *luuuv* her gift. It's lying.

Miss Jeanne: No one is saying you have to lie to express gratitude for gifts you receive that aren't to your taste. Insincerity can be just as obvious as ingratitude.

Brideweena: So how am I supposed to behave when I open Aunt Fifi's gift? At Cousin Stephanie's shower, Aunt Fifi was practically hovering over her like a vulture waiting to watch her open that gift.

Miss Jeanne: The secret is to make the giver the object of your gratitude, not the gift. To do this requires a readjustment of priorities to elevate the status of the giver as more important than the gift. When the gift is really heinous, the immediate reaction should be to turn your attention from the gift and focus it on the giver by noting their kindness and generosity.

Brideweena: So I should tell Aunt Fifi what?

Miss Jeanne: Come on, I think you can figure this out if you try hard enough.

Brideweena (knitting her dainty brow in furrows of concentration)**:** "Oh, Aunt Fifi! They must have taken you hours to make! You are so kind to take the time to make these for me. I appreciate the effort you so lovingly put into all your gifts."

Miss Jeanne: That's a good start. Besides, you might end up loving them. I hear they make great dog chew toys.

Rule 6: Thou Shalt Keep Thy Nose out of the Details

I told Camille that although I couldn't attend her destination wedding in the Bahamas I would love to throw her a shower. She said she understood, and that a lot of people weren't going to be able to come, in-cluding many family members from both the groom's and bride's sides of the family. About eight weeks before the shower, she called me to make some plans. I had planned on getting the invitations out right after Christmas, which was about a week away, and would have been a good six weeks before the shower. She started screaming, and I literally mean screaming, that we needed to get those invitations out and it had to be today!!! And how could I cause her so much stress before her wedding, didn't I care about her, and I was a terrible friend. I should have backed out at this point.

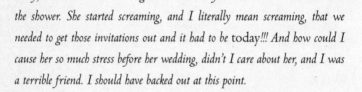

The bride is the guest of honor at any shower held for her. "Guest of honor" is not bridalspeak for "Imperial Grand Princess Who Gets to Micromanage Every Detail." Guests of honor do not stick their prying little noses into the party plans, they don't issue bridal edicts as to how shower plans should appropriately honor them, and they do not crassly manipulate the hostess to get what they want when they want it.

Your "job description" as guest of honor at your own shower is to provide the hostess with a current list of people invited to the wedding, offer suggestions if asked for them (and only if asked!), and behave like an appreciative, humble person in the presence of gift-bearing friends.

Rule 7: Heinous Hostesses Can Test Your Patience

I had two "friends" at the time, and asked one to be maid of honor and one to be a bridesmaid in my wedding. Since I had gone to a commuter college (not a school teeming with social activity), these were my only close girlfriends, but I was so grateful to have them and happy to share this special time with them. Or so I thought. And I was really delighted when the maid of honor, Denise, immediately offered to give me a bridal shower. What a wonderful friend, I thought, especially since we'd only known each other a couple of years. I think that was my first big mistake—to let someone I didn't know very well be my maid of honor. I was content to have a small shower (no more than twenty ladies) and keep it inexpensive, since that's all they could afford. I totally didn't have a problem with that.

So a couple of months before the wedding, the three of us started talking about the shower, and I really thought some kind of theme would be fun and I kept offering suggestions, but they would just giggle and roll their eyes. Then they got together without me and decided to "surprise" me. Oh, boy—that should have clued me in right there. I had no idea what they were cooking up, but I trusted them. They were my "friends." They wouldn't do anything to embarrass me, right? WRONG!

I arrived at the shower, and it was in a small meeting room of a hotel that my bridesmaid worked at as a sales representative. They had put up a few streamers and there was a small table of food, which was fine.

Anyway, I got there and there was a rack of skanky lingerie and some cosmetics displayed that I don't even remember the brand. I was informed that they were going to have a joint "show" at my shower, and guests were told on the invitations to give me money to buy these products I didn't use and certainly didn't want. I couldn't believe they would do this to me. I would have rather not had a shower at all than go through what I was about to go through.

Some people actually were kind enough to bring gifts of beautiful, tasteful lingerie (items that were on my bridal registry). But most brought checks or cash as gifts, which was very awkward, considering I didn't want to cooperate with my bridesmaid's "scheme." I was feeling very angry and very used at this point, so at the end of the shower, when most everybody was gone, I told the sales representatives that I wasn't interested in buying anything at this time. They just looked at me with their mouths open. I cried all the way home from the shower, and my mother was livid after she found out I didn't know a thing about any of their plans. How tacky!!! I ended up using the money I was given from our shower toward our honeymoon at Disney World, which worked out beautifully, even though it peeved my bridesmaids. When I wrote thank-you notes, I told each guest I was not expecting the shower to be arranged this way and that it was a surprise to me to have vendors there, so I was using the cash for our honeymoon. Nobody had a problem with that, and I was glad. It was the only solution I could come up with at the time, and I don't regret it.

If you haven't known your bridesmaids at least five years, don't use them as bridesmaids. It's no guarantee of a successful wedding, but in my opinion, it helps. If I had it to do over again, I'd have no bridesmaids. Later I found out my mom's friend would have hosted my shower. Learn from my mistakes, brides and bridesmaids alike.

Sometimes it happens that a shower hostess has decidedly different tastes than the bride. Sometimes those tastes can merely be a difference in preference such as liking to play silly shower games versus preferring to not play any games at all. On such trivial matters of preference, whatever your shower hostess decides, you should follow suit and enjoy the activities or lack thereof.

However, some shower hostesses' idea of a good time is either a quickie little moneymaking scheme for themselves or an incredibly crass obsession on the paraphernalia of sexual intercourse. Both expose a selfish preoccupation with what pleases the hostess while offering the maximum amount of embarrassment to the bride. Numerous brides write me of their horror at finding out the shower that their supposedly close friends chose to plan involved a considerable amount of preoccupation with a certain part of the male anatomy, or worse, subjected the bride to having a male stripper dance for her, which she found offensive.

The questions the bride should be asking herself are, "How did I end up associating myself with people who seem to not know me at all?" or, "How did I end up associating myself with people who *know* I would hate this yet are inflicting it on me anyway?" Weddings can certainly be crucibles by which the dross of superficiality is burned away and people discover the true nature of those whom they have called "friend." In every instance of others hiring strippers that I have known of in my life, either male or female strippers, the not-so-discreet motivation of those planning this surprise was to embarrass the guest of honor to death. It usually works. It certainly puts the guest of honor in the awkward position of having to tolerate this affront in the name of being a "good sport." If you have friends like this, it may be time to raise your standards and understand friendship as something that edifies and doesn't humiliate.

In some situations, the bride is faced with the dilemma of upholding personal convictions versus being kind to those who are misguided in what they think will please her. The bride in the story above handled the awkward shower as best she could. In more egregious dilemmas, however, a more assertive approach may be called for.

When you discover that a male stripper will be the entertainment, it is perfectly acceptable first to appeal discreetly to the shower hostess and tell her that you would not find this pleasant. If she charges ahead with the plans and the dancer's gyrations are about to commence, it is okay to interrupt the display to appeal to the larger audience. Since the stripper probably brought his own boom box, give an accomplice the duty of finding it and turning it off while you make your appeal. Here's what you could say:

Ladies, I appreciate the efforts you've made to give me a fun party, but I have to confess that this isn't my kind of fun. You are sweet to want to make me happy, but honestly, I'd be happier and more comfortable if this guy weren't here. I'd really rather have a chance to visit with you than watch some stranger shake his booty. How 'bout we go out for some coffee?

If that fails and mob rule prevails, sit on your hands with your eyes closed in silent protest. At least Grandma Finkle's sense of mortification will be assuaged by the knowledge that her granddaughter had no involvement in this embarrassment.

I am aware that some people would consider this an extremely rude slap at the hostess, but consider for a moment. The offense was really committed by the hostess who, despite an appeal, had no consideration for whether she would be offending the bride and her family. We are not obligated to be doormats when confronted with rude, boorish people who seek to use us for personal gratification. It is not uncivil to confront the boorishness, politely, but head-on.

Rule 8: Just Because It Has a Pulse Doesn't Mean It Has to Be Invited

I thought I had seen everything until I attended a friend's shower. She and her fiancé are both of Southern European descent and apparently showers are un-heard-of in the old country. My friend and her family, therefore, made no bones about creating their own brand of "etiquette" to suit their needs.

First of all, both the mother of the bride and mother of the groom hosted the shower, cramming 180 women into this basement banquet hall (maxi-mum gift intake for minimum cost). As the guests arrived, the bride greeted them at the door dressed to the nines. I handed her my gift and she tossed it down the line from one bridesmaid to the next, down to the maid of honor, who ripped open the package and placed the half-opened gift on a table next to the others. As I stood there with my mouth hanging open, I was asked by an-other attendant to take my seat as they wanted to get the five-course meal started. When I asked about what the deal was with the gifts, I was told that with so many women in attendance, they were trying to be expedient and save time . . . no need to bother the bride to open all those gifts and thank everyone as she goes.

The bride and her eight attendants took their seats at the "head table." After the mediocre meal was finally finished, the bridesmaids handed out nicely wrapped favors to all the guests and we were advised that the shower was over. The bride waved good-bye as we left. Not surprisingly, I never did receive a thank-you note for the $80 gift I had given. I was later told by a bridesmaid that "we" (members of their ethnic group) don't send thank-you cards; that they give "expensive" favors instead. They weren't kidding about making up their own rules of etiquette!

Just because you have a large guest list for the wedding does not mean every one of these people needs to be invited to a shower. Showers are supposed to be intimate gatherings of family and close friends. When moderation of shower size goes out the window, the hostesses must resort to an assembly line to expedite the gift opening or else the shower can drag on and on and on. This is no longer a shower; it's a monsoon deluge and the guests rightfully feel that they've been soaked for their gifts.

This story illustrates the point that even if they are fed a substantial meal and given some sort of token favor, people still want some care, consideration, and gratitude for the gift they have chosen to bestow upon the bride. Justifying an impersonal, mechanical approach as an equal trade of meal and favor for a wedding gift doesn't sit well with guests, who are likely to avoid any future showers in your honor.

Rule 9: Guests Don't Cater

Martin and Shelly are two friends of my fiancé. We received their bridal shower invitation for a "Jack and Jill" shower at the home of Shelly's friend Rhonda. Like all good guests are supposed to, we RSVP'd right away and purchased a gift from their registry. Some days later, my fiancé ran into Shelly at her place of work. She asked if we were still coming to the shower. He said, yes, of course, and she told him the shower was BYOB. I guess he must have appeared surprised, because she asked him, "It wasn't on the invitation?" He told me about that little bit of information later in the day, and maybe we're wrong, but we both felt that guests shouldn't have to supply their own refreshments for a bridal shower. I mean, what's next, guests bringing sack lunches to the wedding? I'm sure a lot of people think that having a BYOB bridal shower is okay, but we think it's pretty tacky.

Geez Louise, people are bringing shower gifts and they are also getting bilked for the cost of their own refreshments? Dang, that's tacky. Really, really tacky. If you haven't noticed yet, there is a consistent theme throughout the www.etiquettehell.com Web site and this book. That is that guests should never feel obligated to open their wallets to pay for things that traditionally are the responsibility of a gracious host to provide.

Rule 10: Resist the Nastiest Shower Game of All

Fast-forward to the evening of the bridal shower. Rosa the hostess announced to one and all: "Y'all need to grab an envelope and put your address on it so all Lisa has to do is put the card in it and mail it."

While my fiancé and I were mortified, some of the guests responded with verbal appreciation, uttering comments like, "How sweet!" The rest of the evening we stalled doing this, but the hostess kept hounding guests with, "I don't have your envelope yet," so we finally acquiesced.

Yesterday I received Lisa and Steve's thank-you note. At least they were prompt. Just when I thought I was calmed down about addressing our own thank-you envelope, there it was, and I got agitated all over again.

Miss Jeanne, please help spread the word that making guests address their own thank-you envelopes is one of the worst violations of taste that has become so widespread today. Ugh. End of rant.

I'm only too happy to spread the word about this increasingly popular, and ever boorish, way of weaseling out of spending time writing personal thank-you notes!

While the hostess is often the one who inflicts this atrocity on guests, the bride is nearly always complicit in it. Who do you think supplied the thank-you note envelopes, after all? This represents a sloppy, lazy attitude of ingratitude toward those who have spent time finding a gift, purchasing it, wrapping it, and then transporting it to the shower. Shower gifts cost money. Money is congealed sweat—the hours of labor someone poured forth to be able to purchase the gift. God forbid Queen Bridezilla should have to raise a limp wrist to address the thank-you note envelopes herself, so guests get corralled into doing this as part of a purported shower game or door-prize drawing. Snookered guests willingly go along with this either because they are inwardly delighted that this precedent can be used later to weasel out of their own thank-you note addressing obligations or because, in a wedding version of the Stockholm syndrome, they are coming to love their captors.

Don't try to disguise this as a shower game either:

As people started coming in, I finished my hostessing chores and made my way to the foyer to help greet guests with the bride, Donna. I noticed as each guest went to the table to make a nametag, Donna was having them write their name and address on an envelope, and on the inside flap, a number. Puzzled, I went over to see what was going on. Donna informed me that she had placed a jar of jelly beans on the nametag table. She told her guests that she was having a "Guess the Number of Jellybeans" contest. The people wrote their guess on the flap and put their name and address on the front. In other words, they addressed their own thank-you notes. The "winner" of the game got to keep the jellybeans. I was beyond mortified.

Rule 11: Family Doesn't Host ... Except ...

Whether your family can host a shower for you or not is a topic of much contention with some Etiquette Hell fans. Most people realize this is a breach of etiquette, but justify it by claiming it is "done and generally accepted" in "most" areas of the United States. The "everyone does it" argument doesn't cut it. "If fifty million people say a foolish thing, it is still a foolish thing," said Anatole France. Unkindness is still unkind and greed is still greedy, even if "everyone" is engaging in it. Be bigger than that.

The European and Asian fans of the Etiquette Hell Web site are baffled by the American attitude that a shower is a "must-have" wedding experience. Gift showers are not part of most of the world's wedding customs, including those of the British, but somehow people enjoy their wedding festivities without feeling deprived. Yet even hint to an American bride that a shower may not be in the plans and hysterical wails bemoaning cruel deprivation prompt Mom to take action so that her baby princess is not permanently scarred for life.

The story below exemplifies why a shower hosted by family is an expression of greed, no matter how many decorations are used to hide it:

I'd been engaged for a year when one of my best friends and former college roommates announced that she, too, had just become engaged. Of course, I was ecstatic at the news and excited to be able to share what I'd learned in my own wedding-planning process. Because she'd been such a dear friend and confidante, I offered to throw her a shower if no one else had requested the honor. With much joy and gratitude, she accepted my offer.

Months before her wedding, I contacted her to ask what sort of theme she wanted for the shower. I knew both she and her fiancé already had established households, and I wanted to know what she needed most—kitchen items, bathroom accessories, etc.—to use that as the theme for the day. It was only one of many ideas we talked about for hours as we dreamed up the shower plans. After hanging up with her, I felt wonderful at being able to do this for my best friend.

That was on a Monday. On Wednesday, she called to ask for my new mailing address. When I asked her what for, in a big rush she tells me that her future mother-in-law is hosting a giant wedding shower for her, has rented a very upscale golf course clubhouse, and now needs her to track down as many names and addresses as she can so that invitations can be mailed out as soon as possible. It is still many months to her actual wedding day, but for reasons I still don't know, the shower had to take place very soon. In a state of shock, I gave her my address, but I never got a chance to ask what was going on because she told me she had a "million other people's" addresses to get.

A few days later when I'd calmed down, I called her up and asked her to explain herself. Why was her future mother-in-law giving her a shower when I'd already made plans with her to host one myself? She told me her mother-in-law had proposed the idea of a shower the very day they became engaged. I asked her then why did she agree to have me host it? She replied she was having three, as her own mother (and also matron of honor) was throwing her one, and she didn't see anything wrong with having three. I told her no, there isn't, if different guests were invited to each one. But no! She was planning on inviting the same people to all three! At that point, I politely declined my offer to host a shower for her and proposed a bridesmaids' luncheon instead. Obviously hurt and mystified by my actions, she agreed.

I attended the shower at the country club with a fellow bridesmaid. It was a catered affair and certainly more than I could have afforded to give her. She received many beautiful gifts of Waterford crystal, gold and silver candlesticks,

handblown one-of-a-kind martini sets, etc. I felt a little out of place with my
food processor, but that's not important. What galled me to this day was her
mother passing out flyers *for the next shower—a "tool time" affair even*

The Wedding Consultation

Ethell: When I got married twenty-five years ago, I had no shower. I had a very small wedding and my bridesmaids were my two sisters. I really wish I'd had one and I feel like I missed out on a fun bridal experience. You only get one chance.

Miss Jeanne: You poor thing! There was no engagement party, rehearsal dinner, bridesmaids' luncheon, dress shopping with your sisters, or a wedding reception?

Ethell: Oh, yes, yes! I had all that.

Miss Jeanne: Let me get this straight. You enjoyed numerous wedding-related activities and events yet because of the lack of a shower, you've spent twenty-five years nursing your feelings of deprivation?

Ethell: No one offers to throw showers anymore so I think a family member, not wanting to see the bride disappointed, should take on the responsibility. Where's the harm in this?

Miss Jeanne: My mother used to say, "We are not disappointed because we received too little but rather because we expected too much." Disappointment is the result of presuming to be owed something that one has not received. Sorry, but a shower is not a "right" that a bride or her family can expect as a mandatory part of the wedding experience. Besides, aren't you busy with planning the bridesmaids' luncheon?

though the bride and groom have a cramped condo and no room for a lot of bulky tools. The bride confided to me that this was "the only way for her to get all the gifts they needed." She announced to the room after the flyers were passed out that she and the groom would be registering at the local hardware store, so would people please wait a few days before purchasing their gifts!

I haven't decided whether I'm attending the second shower out of a sense of obligation or not. She's a bridesmaid in my own wedding, and because I still love her dearly, I don't want any more awkwardness than there already is. But secretly, I'm dreading the experience. I just pray to the heavens above, no further flyers are passed out!

Family-hosted showers might seem fine to you on first examination. However, think more deeply about the conflict of interest involved here. A family member hosting a shower is arranging the enrichment of his or her own extended family by raking in goodies from others to ensure a family member is suitably outfitted for marriage. It benefits the entire family, especially the parents of the happy couple, to have a well-established new family unit that they did not personally have to expend resources to achieve. Mom, therefore, has a strong stake in making sure son or daughter is appropriately showered with gifts. As the story notes, the series of showers has become an organized crime spree by family collusion to extort the greatest amount of booty possible from the guests.

Adam's sister, Janet, wanted to give me a bridal shower. Thank goodness, she offered and didn't try to "surprise" me. I consider it improper for relatives or relatives-to-be to give showers. I tried to explain this to her gently and politely, and she brushed me off with "well, times have changed" and "everybody does it up here." I told her firmly, no, thank you, and got off with the excuse that a longtime neighbor was already hosting one and all the same people Janet would have invited were already coming to that one. Disaster averted!

The only exception to "family does not host the shower" is when *only* family is invited. Sometimes these "showers" are more about introducing the bride to the groom's family than about gifts, but once it is called a "shower," the understanding in guests' minds is that gifts are expected.

Brideweena's Checklist

1. Have I given a list of the wedding guests to the shower hostesses?

2. Have I resisted all temptations to dictate my preferences for the way the shower is planned?

3. Have I practiced saying, "Thank you! That was so sweet of you!" for when I'm opening the fifth toaster?

4. Have I copied this chapter of the book and given it to Muffin Louise to read before she plans the shower?

5. Did I remember to accept Muffin Louise's mother's offer to host the shower before Mom gets too many ideas?

SIX

On Ceremony We Stand

The music at a wedding procession always reminds me of the
music of soldiers going into battle. —HEINRICH HEINE

ONWARD WEDDING SOLDIERS, MARCHING as to... what?
Will your attendants march grim-faced down the aisle as a final duty to fulfill to She Who Wears the White? Are your future in-laws approaching the wedding ceremony as if trudging to the
guillotine? Have your flower girls taken on the appearance of splay-
legged mules desperately not wanting even to enter the church? Maybe
it's a good idea to assess your ceremony plans.

The temptation you will experience is one of believing all those
bridal magazines when they trumpet, "It's *your* special day!" It seems
so logical. You are the one getting married, so shouldn't everyone ac-
quiesce to your plans for the perfect wedding? The reality is that none
of us lives in a vacuum devoid of relationships, and weddings are a lit-
eral cacophony of relational interactions. If you ask people to participate in the wedding ceremony, there has to be some consideration
given to their personal comfort.

Weddings turn some people into nutcases who inflict things on friends and family in ways they wouldn't dream of in any other context. Your friends and family will likely go along with any goofy idea you come up with merely to keep the peace. But why be known as the person who involved her loved ones in a debacle that will go down in the annals of local folklore? The goal should be a unique but tasteful wedding that achieves your objectives while balancing considerations for guests, family, the bridal party, and vendors.

In the grand scheme of life, the little planning details that you agonized over into the wee hours of the night won't be remembered by people within a week of your wedding. But screw them over with some presumptuous rudeness and they will enshrine you in their memory for eons.

Rule 1: Let's Get This Thing Started on Time

The invitation should have been the first clue that this wedding was going to be a Wedding from Hell. Enclosed with the standard engraved invitation was a badly typed list of instructions, beginning with the admonition that "the wedding vows will be tightly timed to coincide with the sun's apogee so please be on time as the wedding will begin at precisely 1:00 P.M.*"*

The appointed day arrived and we set off for the state park where the wedding was to be held. It was about an hour and a half away so we left at about ten thirty in order to make sure that we were there on time as the invitation demanded. We arrived at the park around eleven forty-five and it's a good thing that we did because we couldn't find any posted signs or directions to the exact location of the wedding! We ended up driving around the campground for almost half an hour before we finally stumbled upon the location of the wedding.

It was nearly one and we were all expecting the wedding to begin promptly as the bride and groom had stated so urgently in the invitation. One o'clock came, and nothing appeared to be happening. One fifteen came, then one thirty, and finally one of the groomsmen wandered up to the "staging cabin," where the bride and bridesmaids were getting ready, to find out what was going on. He came back to report that "the bride was putting the finishing touches on her costume" and it would start soon.

Two o'clock came, and went. The groom was standing around chatting with guests. Finally, at two thirty, the wedding planner/photographer came scuttling down the hill to tell us that the bride was ready to begin.

Contrary to whatever old adage you heard, it is not fashionable to be late to your own wedding. It's grossly rude to everyone—guests, wedding party, officiant, and vendors. It shouldn't be presumed that guests have so much time on their hands that they can sit around waiting for you to finish primping yourself to perfection. By the time your wedding does start, their foul mood will negatively color their perception of your stunning loveliness anyway, making your preparations all for naught. Ugly is as ugly does.

Timing a wedding ceremony to begin with the sun's apogee? Well, that's a new one on me. I wonder what cosmic realignment occurred when the wedding did not commence at the celestially advantageous moment. Along those same lines of silly traditions, I did have a person write to tell me of a wedding she attended in which the bride wanted the vows to coincide with the upsweep of the minute hands from the half hour, based on a superstition that the upsweep is a positive omen of a good wedding whereas making vows on the downsweep of the minute hands from the hour foretells bad luck. Something occurred to cause a delay in the scheduled start time, but rather than starting as soon as possible, the bride made everyone wait a full hour for the minute hand of the clock once again to be on the upsweep from the half hour. There was a glaring bad omen for the marriage, all right, but it had nothing to do with a silly superstition about clocks.

Rule 2: Don't Deprive Thy Guests of a Place to Park the Caboose

The ceremony took place at a golf course, a very beautiful location but with only enough chairs for about twenty of her seventy guests to sit in, so the rest of us stood through the ceremony, which was long. Plus not only could we not see the ceremony through all the people standing in front of us, we could not hear the ceremony, either, due to the loud country music blaring in the backyard of a nearby house.

After the ceremony everyone went through the receiving line, offered their congratulations, and then the wedding party went off to have their pictures taken. The pictures were taken at the golf course. At first it was pleasant to watch. Because the reception was to take place at the same location, watching the pictures being taken was about all you could do. Unfortunately, though, standing in the hot sun for two hours didn't remain pleasant. Now I get that the pictures are important and I don't begrudge them the two hours they took, however once again they should have looked into the importance of seating. The reception dinner that was taking place inside was not open to the guests until halfway through the picture-taking process so the only place to sit was at a few patio tables; needless to say not enough for everyone to sit.

Yes, I know that little chapel in the woods is positively rustically adorable and perfectly fits your romantic vision of the sublime wedding-ceremony location. But what will it be like for your guests to sit there in ninety-eight-degree heat because there is no air-conditioning, or worse, have to stand for more than a hour during the ceremony? Guests shouldn't be viewed as your personal fan club willing to endure hours of metatarsal torture just to get a glimpse of your royal loveliness floating down the aisle and then view an assortment of wedding-party backsides during the ceremony. At least let them sit in relative comfort if they have to endure that visual treat.

Immutable Fact of Life

Be chintzy with the seating and your guests will be chintzy in their estimations of your hospitality talents. Very chintzy.

Rule 3: Theme Weddings Can Be a Nightmare

My fiancé was to be a groomsman in his cousin's wedding. His cousin was the groom. The wedding was to be outdoors at eleven A.M. at the bride's family home (a beautiful area on a hill with a grand view). My fiancé picked up his tux Thursday night and showed it to me. Silver-gray western cut with yellow cummerbund and tie. I thought it wasn't the most attractive style or combination of colors, and the overall effect reminded me vaguely of something else (I didn't figure it out until later), but I figured if it made the bride happy, then so what? I knew a tux that early in the day was a faux pas, but hey, it was her wedding.

As I had to work Friday, I missed the Friday-afternoon rehearsal and met up with my fiancé that night at the casual, outdoors barbecue dinner (also at the bride's house). I could see that a very pretty gazebo had been built for the ceremony and many potted plants, trees, and flowers brought in. My fiancé told me that I was in for a "treat" the next day and that he could not believe what they planned to do, but he would not explain what he meant except to start laughing whenever he thought about it.

The wedding site looked very pretty Saturday morning. White chairs were set up for the guests and white ribbons were hanging from the gazebo and trees. As the music started playing, I noticed that it was all old, Southern tunes ("Dixie" was the only one missing). There really was a little antebellum feeling in the air.

The music changed to "My Old Kentucky Home." Then came the seating of the mothers. First the groom's mother was escorted to her seat, followed closely by the groom's father who wore the silver-gray western tux but with tails (and from his expression and posture he seemed to understand that it was far too early to be dressed that way). She wore a dark, solid green dress with a heavy brocade jacket and flowing, calf-length skirt. Her only jewelry was a pair of simple gold earrings. She was stunning. She, too, looked a bit sheepish, however. In a moment I found out why.

The bride's mother came next.

She was wearing a solid white, floor-length, hoop-skirted dress that looked as if it were yanked out of some old movie depicting the Civil War era— except hers was much more ornate and had crescent folds (much like curtain swags) going down the skirt with large fabric roses at each upswing of the folds. Her hair was in the biggest, poofy helmet style. She had gaudy rings on her fingers and dangling rhinestones in her ears. She was beaming. I was not the only guest who gasped. Some whispered, "Oh, my God!" The groomsmen filed into the gazebo with the groom, who also wore the silver-gray western-style tails tux. My fiancé caught my eye, smiled, and winked. Suddenly I realized what the gray reminded me of: It was the color of the uniforms of Confederate soldiers.

The music changed again, and the theme song from Gone with the Wind *started playing.*

Down the aisle came the bridesmaids. Each was wearing a huge, hoop-skirted, floor-length yellow dress with a broad-brimmed yellow garden-party hat and yellow lace gloves. Their bodices had the look of sequined tube tops, but a shawl of yellow organza covered their shoulders. All seven swayed down the aisle, giving the full, swinging bell effect to their skirts. Then came the bride.

The bride's gown was a white hoop-skirted ordeal that had more ruffles and crystals and pearls and lace and bows and organza than are carried in the average fabric store. Who knows what, if any, pattern was supposed to be represented on the skirt, as there was too much stuff on it to allow such discernment. The satin train—trimmed in bows—somehow attached to the waist and made it over the skirt to flow a good fifteen feet behind the bride. It, too, was overly decorated with sparkly beads and pearls. The sleeves gave her the shoulders of a football linebacker, while the front plunged so low, she may as well have been topless. The bride's entire head was masked by yards and yards of tulle on a crown of white silk flowers and rhinestones. How she saw through it all, I still wonder. The overall effect was of a fairy godmother whose wand had exploded at a glitter factory.

Her father had to have known that a beerbelly that large should never be allowed to hang out of the cut of a tailcoat, and that a cummerbund is insufficient to act as a girdle.

By the time this parade had finished, half of the guests were covering their mouths to stifle their laughs. Unfortunately, their shaking shoulders gave them away. I kept thinking that there had to be a hidden camera somewhere and that any minute someone would jump out and say we all were on Candid Camera.

The ceremony had three solos in it (all current love songs), but otherwise was fairly short. After the minister pronounced them husband and wife, I imagined the bride raising her fist and crying, "With God as my witness, I shall never be single again." One bridesmaid stole the moment by swooning, literally back of the hand on the forehead with knees buckling straight downward, thus causing some commotion as three young men came to her rescue and made her sit down in the front row. We finally heard "Dixie," as it was played for the recessional.

The word "abundant" does not do justice to the reception. It was in another section of the yard and spilled into the house. Country music blared and the keg beer flowed. There was even a punch fountain into which someone had tried to pour beer—the result was a large, frothy mess. Many guests got loud and drunk. Half the guests went wild each time the Cotton-Eyed Joe was played. Condoms filled with shaving cream and vulgar expressions of copulation were the main decor for the couple's car. I truly expected to see the Confederate flag flying somewhere. Thankfully it wasn't. It was on the bride's garter, however.

Through it all the groom's poor parents smiled, but their eyes revealed the discomfort and embarrassment that was just behind those smiles. I was born, raised, and still live in a former Confederate state, so I am not some "Yankee" laughing at Southern style. This simply was one of the most "memorable" events I have ever attended.

I can only add to this story that the groom was just as stunned as everyone else by the mother's and the bride's dresses. The bride's family is very country in its attitude, but has never been tacky before. My husband's cousin later told us that his mother-in-law chose the white dress because she felt that her own wedding was nothing (they eloped) and wanted to "feel" like a bride this time. The bride reportedly gasped when she saw the photographer's proofs and now is embarrassed about her own dress being so over-the-top and revealing. She loves Gone with the Wind and, along with her mother, thought the theme wedding would be beautiful and unique. She now regrets it.

The Etiquette Hell position on theme weddings is generally to discourage over-the-top theme weddings since the emphasis can too easily be diverted from the solemnity of the ceremony to becoming a theatrical production that diminishes the sanctity of the event. Not to mention that your guests can be diverted from focusing on witnessing the vows to visually absorbing every second of the spectacle so they can relate the gory details to their friends. Adorn yourself and the bridal party in full *Star Trek* regalia, including Klingons in full makeup, and your guests may wonder if there is no intelligent life at the wedding and they need to be beamed up.

If extensive costuming and makeup are needed to don a persona, much like an actor dons stage makeup to assume a role, who is getting married? The persona created by the heavy makeup or the real person who happens to be assuming a persona for the event? Marriage should never be entered into frivolously, and an overabundance of role-playing makes it seem more like a theatrical event than a wedding. A wedding ceremony highlights a serious public vow in which two people undertake to spend a lifetime together building a family. This isn't a game.

Rule 4: Ceremony Music Should Be Appropriate

One of my cousins decided that "Here Comes the Bride" wasn't right for her wedding processional. She wanted "some classical music." Heaven knows where she looked, because come her wedding day, she was marched down the aisle by her father to a very beautiful piece of music . . ., instantly recognizable to everyone there as the theme from The Godfather.

Odd choices in ceremony music aren't likely to offend the average guest but they can increase the odds that the "snicker factor" will kick in. Guess what everyone will be talking about during the reception?

Some churches forbid secular music as well as wedding classics such as the "Wedding March" being played during wedding ceremonies, so check beforehand with the church's wedding director about the policy. There are also people who believe the atmosphere of the wedding ceremony should be consistent with the seriousness of the commitment being entered into. That doesn't mean they are killjoys out to wring every bit of humor from your wedding. It just means that their sense of propriety and decorum leads them to make a connection between sight and sound.

Rule 5: Don't Use a Guest Hierarchy

When I received my invitation to the wedding of a family friend last summer, I was surprised to see a small insert in the invitation. The insert was about the size of a business card and it said, "You are invited to sit within the ribbon."

I had no idea what this meant, but I soon found out.

When I arrived at the wedding, I saw that a large section in the middle of the sanctuary had been roped off by attaching a thick pink ribbon to the outside of the pews. When guests arrived, the ushers asked each guest if they had been invited to sit "within the ribbon" and seated them accordingly. It wasn't just family that was invited to sit within the ribbon—it was a wide array of people.

When the wedding started, the minister welcomed everyone and said that the bride and groom would especially like to welcome those seated within the ribbon.

He went on to explain that the guests seated within the ribbon had been special and important in the bride's and groom's lives, so they wanted to honor them.

So I guess that everyone outside of the ribbon wasn't all that special or important to them? I bet if some of the guests had known beforehand that they meant nothing to the bride and groom, they wouldn't have shelled out money for a gift or even bothered attending! I thought that this was in extremely bad taste.

Seating within the ribbon is an acceptable way of making sure family and very close friends don't end up seated in some dank corner in the rear of the church, particularly when the guest list is quite large. It is also exceedingly helpful when the ushers are naïve college students with no clue as to what they are doing.

But "seating within the ribbon" can become a pretentious way of crassly singling out guests, as was done in this wedding. It should be reserved only for close family and very close friends and *never* used as a social hierarchy. Just because Mrs. Fumpledink is the richest, most powerful person in your hamlet, that alone does not qualify her as "within the ribbon" material. Mentioning the guests seated within the ribbon as part of the wedding ceremony is just plain crass because it is stating the obvious and really rubbing it in.

Rule 6: This Isn't a Funeral

Susan's older sister has been married for several years, and their father sang "Sunrise, Sunset" at her wedding ceremony. Sadly, he passed away about two years before Susan's wedding. During her ceremony they stopped cold, right in the middle of the exchange of vows, and presented a ten-minute slide show memorializing her father while her extremely tone-deaf brother-in-law grunted his way through "Sunrise, Sunset." They ended the slide show with a photo of Susan's dead father in his casket. It was one of the most morbid, inappropriate things I've ever seen, and I still wonder why they would include that in their wedding!

Once the prohibition against mixing death with weddings is breached, morbid displays of displaced affection arise like a bad nightmare. Wedding guests are not there to partake in your public displays of grief, or witness a memorial service. It simply isn't fair to ambush unsuspecting guests who think they were invited to celebrate a wedding. Some people have written to me of feeling assaulted afresh with grief to have tangible and obvious references to the deceased mentioned in a wedding when they least suspect it.

Don't underestimate your own reaction to an obvious memorial to a deceased parent. Weddings are a very emotional time even under the happiest of circumstances, and faced with a heartrending reminder of a loved one's absence, it is not unlikely that you could react more emotionally than expected. The middle of your wedding ceremony is not the time to dissolve into sobs of grief.

I know the death of a beloved one who cannot be there to witness your wedding is a tragic loss. No one is suggesting you forget a deceased father or mother or grandparent on one of the most special of days in your life as if they never existed. You can have tasteful, and intimately appropriate, remembrances sprinkled throughout your wedding day and ceremony. Some people have laid a single rose on the seat where the missing person would have sat or at the altar. Wear a favorite piece of jewelry, or carry their favorite Bible. Discreetly place a framed photo of the deceased (just not in the casket, please) in the reception venue. One touching suggestion I heard was to place the bride's bouquet on the deceased's grave in a private moment between the ceremony and reception. Or have one candle dedicated to the memory of the deceased which a family member discreetly lights just before the ceremony is to begin.

Rule 7: Don't Abuse the Singers

Barbee and I have been best friends since junior high and were long ago adopted into each other's families, so I was touched but not particularly surprised when her younger sister Adele told me that she was engaged and wanted me to be the soloist at her wedding. I, of course, immediately agreed. I was a little surprised when she had me buy an attendant's dress (identical to the bridesmaids', but in a different color), but did so without complaint.

This was in August 2001. She told me that the wedding would be in June 2002, so I had nearly a year to prepare. Adele assured me that she trusted me, so I should choose a song on my own. The only guidance I had was "a popular country song." (The wedding was in Texas. Most of the wedding songs were country.) I agreed and spent several months searching for the perfect song. I finally found what I felt was the perfect song and e-mailed her my choice. (I live several states away.) Just to be sure, I also included two alternatives and made sure to have full lyrics and sound clips from each choice. This was in late January.

Several weeks went by, and then I finally got a reply from her. "Oh, didn't Barbee tell you? I found someone else to sing. Would you be the guest book attendant instead?" (I doubt she would have even asked that if I hadn't already spent $100 on the dress.) I was floored, insulted, and very disappointed, but accepted graciously. What else could I do? Well, fast-forward several months. I was back down in Texas, up to my neck in details for another wedding, where I was maid of honor. I was horribly stressed about this one, and didn't have much time to worry about Adele's wedding. Well, that is until I got a call from her two days before the first wedding and barely two weeks before hers. It turned out that her preferred other singer had canceled so would I please take over again?

Once again, I was floored, but since I'd already learned the solo, I decided I should go ahead and agree. Well, the next day I received an envelope containing the lyrics to the entirely new song she wanted me to learn. (In two weeks!) This was while I was completely stressed about the other wedding and discovering that the dress Adele had made me order was at least two sizes too small, absolutely couldn't be altered to fit me, and the design had been discontinued so I couldn't get another one!

Well, I couldn't back out at this date, so I spent two straight weeks working hard to learn the new song. It went fairly well. I worked out with the bride a different dress to wear, and made my arrangements to fly in the day before to participate in the rehearsal and meet with my pianist, supplied by the church. I should've known things couldn't work out so well! The pianist was over half an hour late to our rehearsal, leaving less than half an hour before the regular wedding rehearsal was to start. Then she absolutely could not fit her playing to the key and tempo I had learned, and tried to convince me to relearn the entire song the day before the wedding. She wouldn't listen to any of the suggestions I made to work things out, and it took a decree from the bride to finally have her agree to just play the intro and bridge pieces and let me sing unaccompanied. (The one thing I truly appreciated the bride for the whole time!)

That night at the rehearsal dinner, the bride spent quite a long time calling up each and every one of her large bridal party (fourteen attendants, plus flower girls and cousins in various jobs such as guest book attendant and cake cutter) for their thank-you gifts. She gave a short little speech about each of them, such as how they'd met, or how much of a help they'd been during the planning. She didn't leave out anyone, not even the two-year-old flower girl . . . except, of course, me. I'm not a greedy or fame-seeking person, but are a few words of acknowledgment after all the work I'd done too much to ask? (Adele did come up to me ten minutes or so after all of that to give me a gift and explain that she "forgot" to mention me!)

Well, finally the day of the wedding rolled around. First, Barbee and I were rolled out of bed early in the morning to set up the rehearsal hall before heading all the way across town to the salon where the bride and all her other bridesmaids had been getting their hair and makeup done all morning. (All the bridesmaids were sorority sisters, while Barbee was named maid of honor only after the mother of the bride put her foot down.) After a truly hideous hair experience I can't even put into words, Barbee and I headed over to the church to dress and prepare for wedding pictures.

Now, I was supposed to meet with the pianist at four, pictures were at four thirty, and the wedding at six. As I should have expected, the pianist didn't show up until five thirty, about thirty seconds before she was supposed to begin playing the music for guest seating. I was horribly stressed and very upset that we wouldn't have time for even a quick run-through, after all the difficulties we'd had the previous day, so I simply told her I would do the entire song unaccompanied. I wasn't sure if I should just run out screaming by then, but I just smiled my best and waited for the ceremony to begin. Luckily, I seemed to have exhausted the bad-luck bug by then! My solo went beautifully and I had people complimenting me all during the reception. The rest of the wedding went smoothly as well, though truthfully by then I was too exhausted to notice!

This is probably the worst example I've seen of abusing the singer(s), but the elements are applicable for any ceremony. Singers need time to find the sheet music, to practice, and certainly to rehearse with other musicians and the sound system. While many are gifted beyond the talents of mere mortals with singing voices that bring people like me to tears, it would be wrong to assume that they can belt out any old song in front of an audience with little preparation.

The same goes for readers. Give them the text well in advance so they can become familiar with it. Have a care for those who have crossed that threshold of middle age, are in need of bifocals, and may want to make their copy into larger print.

You should either pay the singer(s) for their efforts or, if their singing was a gift to you, write them a glowing, sincere, effusive letter of thanks as soon as your suitcases have been unpacked from the honeymoon.

Following on the heels of singer abuse is musician abuse. . . .

Rule 8: Don't Abuse the Musicians

My husband is a gifted organist. His music teacher tried to convince him to go pro—but he thought that life as a musician would be too unpredictable. But he has kept up his talent.

A few years ago, some friends of ours were getting married and didn't have much money since they were still in med school. My husband offered to play the organ for them for free. (When we got married, we discovered that this service is worth at least $75 to $100 an hour where we live.) Since we are in our late twenties, many of our friends are getting married. They all have many friends who are getting married. After my husband played for our friends, he suddenly had many people asking him to play for their weddings as well. Most of these requests are accompanied by "Well, we can't pay you but . . ." Since my husband is a good-hearted man and he likes to play, he often accepts. So now we receive piles of wedding invitations, sometimes to weddings of complete strangers, so he can play the organ for them.

Since we are invited as guests to the reception, etiquette indicates that we should bring a gift. Our policy is to buy a gift if we are friends with the cou-

ple. But if we don't (or barely) know them, we have decided that his organ playing makes a lovely gift. In this case we only give a card. During the summer months we sometimes get invited to two or three weddings a month—we can't spend that sort of money on strangers!

Most people are happy with this, but I have been called up by distraught brides who want to know where their gift is. They don't accept my explanation because most of the time they have seen us give gifts to close friends. I have been called cheap by a bride who had my husband playing for three hours. I have had one piece of work cry about how she was counting on "people like me" who could afford her $200-a-piece place settings (I can?). I was at a party once where a woman I hardly know pointed out that she couldn't stand people who came to her wedding and didn't pony up enough dough or goods to cover the cost of their food. This was someone who had a punch, cake, and nuts reception and asked my husband to play background music for three hours on the piano. (I still don't know why she counted him as an invited guest.)

Then there was the time we were called by a hysterical bride three hours before the ceremony. She had just noticed that we had RSVP'd "no." (We had something else going on.) It was too bad because she had assumed that he'd realize that he was supposed to play the organ!

As wedding season starts up again, he has learned to say, "I'd love to play as our wedding gift to you." I guess it is true that weddings bring out the rudest in most people!

This story illustrates, for me, the primary reason why no one should presume she is owed anything by anyone. Just because Aunt Deedee has prepared her famous baklava for every family wedding since 1958 or your friends have warbled like Sonny and Cher at all your pals' weddings, that does not mean you should presume they'll be available to do so for your wedding.

It can be awkward to ask someone for a favor of this magnitude.
What you are doing is asking for a very expen-
sive gift and putting them in the awkward position of having to say no. People inherently
dislike saying no to a friend in need so they
will do it at your request even though it may
be something they don't really want to do.
On the other hand, people have expressed
to me their reticence in offering their services to a friend as a gift because they don't
want the bride to feel obligated, or they are
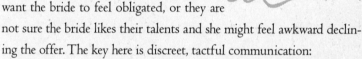
not sure the bride likes their talents and she might feel awkward declin-
ing the offer. The key here is discreet, tactful communication:

> Dexter, I was wondering if you might be available to play the or-
> gan for my wedding? I know you might be busy at this time of
> year so I don't want you to feel obligated.

It would not be appropriate for you even to hint that you want this as
a gift. It's up to the musician to offer his or her talents as a wedding
gift. If they never offer to perform for free as a wedding gift, you need
to then follow up with payment for their services. If those services are
good enough for you to want them for your wedding, they are good
enough for you to pay a fair price for them, and perhaps a little more
in gracious appreciation for their enhancement of your ceremony:

> Dexter, you did such a lovely job at our wedding. The music was
> the perfect accompaniment to the ceremony. I'd like to know what
> I can offer as compensation for such a beautiful performance?

Rule 9: Public Places Aren't Private

My bride-to-be and I are both Renaissance Faire people, and she had always dreamed of having a Renaissance wedding. She also wanted a large wedding. Now, she really has no family, or at least no family that was willing to travel for her wedding, so we agreed to do it in my home state, where I do have a large family. My bride and I were paying for the wedding, which included tickets to the fair, meal coupons from the food booths, beverages for the guests after the wedding, and so forth. The wedding itself was considered "public" and other fairgoers were welcome to attend, but the reception afterward was for guests only.

Now for the ceremony. I proceed to the altar, with my best man, grooms-man, and ringbearer, and await my bride. At this moment, an elderly man (a fairgoer, not an invited guest) walks up to me while I am standing at the altar and proceeds to start complaining about the seat he had. Apparently he had sat in something, and wanted me to stop my wedding and redress his problems! After informing him that I was more concerned with cleaning up the blood that I was about to spill if he did not sit down and shut up, he quietly sat down and behaved himself. I turned to again watch my blissfully unaware bride start her entrance. After her arrival I noticed another fairgoer, in a very bright yellow top, move up behind my bride so that she could get a better view. Through-out the ceremony, this lady was never farther than ten feet from the wedding party, and taking constant pictures, and moving to get the best views! Again, since she was behind her, my bride knew nothing of this, as I struggled to keep a straight face.

The problem with wedding ceremonies in public places is that you truly have no reliable control over spectators or background events. You shouldn't expect privacy in a public area, or consideration from bystanders, for that matter. I'm always amazed at how people think the world should stand still while they have their wedding ceremony in a public park. Dog owners out walking the pooch should stay far away. Kids screaming and laughing on playground equipment are to be silent. You're going to light up a charcoal grill nearby? Over my dead bridal body! Hey, you, with the lawn mower! Move your mower-pushing backside away from my wedding! Keep that Frisbee far from me!

It would be nice if everyone in the world were kind and thoughtful but humankind has not advanced to the point of universally selfless courtesy. So, if there is a mutant Barbarian out there, odds are he'll find your public wedding and act in a manner appropriate to his Barbarism. For you in turn to scream, curse, or flip the bird at these Barbarians in the midst of your wedding ceremony is probably not going to increase the joy of the occasion.

You can have your dream wedding in a public place, but you shouldn't presume that you own the earth and the sky for a mile in every direction. Whatever happens, happens, and the best plan is to be willing to roll with the punches good-naturedly.

Rule 10: Act Your Age

> *My boyfriend was the best man, so before the wedding I was supposed to hang out with the bride's side of the wedding party. The bride and her mother bickered horribly about everything, and the bride sounded just like I did when I was six. "But Maaaaaaaa!"*

That was the mild end of the spectrum. Here's the wild end of the spectrum. . . .

Apparently Jill didn't like anything that was going on during the rehearsal. She screamed at her mom for bringing her brother in late to the rehearsal. (He just flew in and came directly from the airport. His original flight was delayed because of weather.) She had a photographer to capture the "rehearsal moments" and he wasn't taking the pictures she wrote out for him so she screamed at him so badly that not only was it demeaning but everyone was questioning why he didn't just leave. (He also was the photographer for the next day.) She screamed at everyone because they were not "in their places." She yelled at the four-year-old flower girl because she refused to walk down the aisle on cue. (The mother told me that she was too scared from all of the screaming.) Jill also screamed at her MOH and bridesmaids because they hadn't done enough for her and she listed it all: she was upset about the bridal shower, no bachelorette party, they didn't make her the rehearsal bouquet out of the bows from the bridal shower, and it just went on and on and on. She started yelling at the justice of the peace and he tried taking her aside to calm her down but she went off on him and stormed out. She came back five minutes later in a higher level of tirade and started kicking over chairs, and ripping off the ribbons that the bridesmaids and relatives were placing up on the pews. They weren't good enough. Nothing was good enough. And she just didn't stop screaming. The bridesmaids ran out crying, the relatives went outside just to get some air.

The next morning was the wedding. Knowing that I wasn't invited was a relief for me. I had plans to have breakfast with the mother of the groom and my ex-brother-in-law. When I went to pick them up, they told me that Jill didn't want anyone who wasn't a bridesmaid or groomsman to be in the limos. So basically, none of Jill's future in-laws had a ride to the wedding. Just when we started talking about what to do, the mother of the groom got a phone call from Jill. Jill told us that her car was vandalized and there was no battery, and two tires were flat. She had to go get her hair done and the bridesmaids were not answering their phones. (Gee, her car gets vandalized and her bridesmaids aren't answering the phone. What a strange coincidence.) We feel bad and decide to drop her off and wait at a nearby restaurant to have breakfast. With people talking, dishes clanking, and being a few storefronts away, we can hear her screaming at the hairdresser.

If you are old enough to marry, you are old enough not to behave like a child with whining or full-fledged scream-o-rama tantrums. Screaming is verbal abuse. If you are willing to vent your frustrations on friends and family with full-throated vigor, your potential for verbally abusing any future children has to be taken into serious consideration by your future spouse. I wouldn't inflict this bride on a pet hamster. No one may bother to confront you about this kind of misbehavior, instead opting to carry on as if watching a tantalizing horror movie that they can't tear themselves away from. What new and heinous torture will the Bridezilla inflict on her next victim? The silence of the victims and observers, in that case, is not golden, nor is your reputation once you've exceeded the decibel decency level.

The Wedding Consultation

Miss Jeanne: I hear through the wedding grapevine that you let loose with a volley of angry comments earlier this week.

Brideweena: It was after a long day of work . . . I couldn't call any photographers all day . . . my lunch was stolen out of the break room refrigerator . . . the day just sucked. Then I found out that Muffin Louise did not purchase the dyed shoes she was supposed to get by my imposed deadline so I let her have it with both barrels.

Miss Jeanne: Hmm, sounds to me like an exercise in prostrating oneself in abject humility to ask for forgiveness might be in order.

Brideweena: Why should I? Muffin Louise was very wrong to not get this done in a timely fashion and she caused me even more stress than I needed that day. This is *my* day after all, and she should be considerate of the stress this wedding planning is causing me and not pile more on.

Miss Jeanne: Regardless of what anyone else does, you need to take responsibility for your own actions, be the bigger person, and admit to your own faults. Yelling is not the most productive method of getting people to do what you want them to do.

Brideweena: Okay, I'll call her and say, "I am sorry you were offended when I yelled at you for not doing your job!"

Miss Jeanne: Whoa! Let's just nip that in the bud. No blame-shifting allowed when apologizing to people. Just identify your wrongdoing with no embellishments, take responsibility for them, ask for forgiveness, and move on.

Brideweena: You know, Miss Jeanne, you are one cruel woman to insist that I do this. I am a victim of Muffin Louise and deserve some understanding and compassion for my stressed-out nerves.

Miss Jeanne: Get over it.

Rule 11: Don't Abuse the Church

Several years ago, my church lost their sexton and I filled in for a few months until they found someone new. Aside from doing the regular weekly cleaning

and vacuuming, I also had to be there to set up and open the church for weddings.

One Saturday there was a wedding scheduled where neither the bride nor
the groom were members of the church, and they brought their own minister. (I
never did know why they didn't get married at their own church, as I don't
think they or any member of their family had any connection to ours.)

No one ever expects the wedding to start on time, but I figured that since the
wedding was scheduled for four P.M., even allowing extra time for everyone to arrive and get settled, the ceremony, the receiving line, and then straightening and vacuuming the church, there was no reason why I shouldn't be out of there by about
sevenish and so I made an eight o'clock date with my boyfriend to see a movie.

The groom and the minister were there by three thirty, and right on time the
limousine pulled up out front with the bride. My mother and I watched from
the window while she came in with her bridesmaids, which was quite a spectacle, since it was raining that day (not pouring, just a light rain—this fact becomes important later in the story) and it took the drivers of both limousines
and her mother to get her inside without her dress getting wet.

So, the ceremony went on, we heard the organist play the recessional; we
waited a little while for them to do their receiving line and around six o'clock
I went downstairs to start cleaning up. There were still a few guests lingering,
but everyone was starting to clear out. When I walked into the parlor, I noticed
something—on the carpet. I couldn't tell what it was, but it was small and
scattered around and I thought it was probably glitter from the bouquets or
something. No big deal. Then I noticed quite a bit more on the carpet in the
narthex—I was starting to get a little irritated, because I thought this was an
awful lot of glitter to have just shaken loose from the bouquets.

Then I walked into the sanctuary—and the floor, the carpet, the pews, the
altar, everything, was covered in this stuff. Literally covered. You couldn't see
the carpet in some places. Then I realized what it was.

Since it was raining and the guests couldn't stand outside to throw birdseed at the couple as they came down the steps of the church they decided to throw the birdseed at them inside the sanctuary.

Needless to say, these people did not get their deposit back. I had to call my boyfriend to cancel our date since I knew it would take hours to get the mess cleaned up. He (and this is why I married him) went over and borrowed his mother's vacuum cleaner and came over to help my mother and me clean the church. We vacuumed for two solid hours just to get the church presentable for services the next day and then spent a good part of Sunday afternoon vacuuming some more. Months later people were still finding birdseed in some pretty strange places around the church.

And people wonder why many churches no longer permit the throwing of rice or birdseed anywhere on church property. It should go without saying that you should exercise care and consideration in honoring the building-use of policies of your venue. Don't engage in even a hint of presumption by trying to get away with breaking their Rules, so ask the wedding director of the church what the policies are before you get your heart set on swinging a piñata from the church's chandeliers. You don't want to make plans to use Aunt Tildi's antique candelabras on the altar only to discover that the church does not permit open flames.

Set the tone for your attendants and guests as well. I once stopped six college guys from using duct tape to attach a large banner to a hallway wall of the church where the wedding was being held. They hadn't given a second thought to how the paint would look afterward, nor to how the bride and groom would look to the church staff afterward either.

Rule 12: Shame, Shame, the Sham Wedding

> *My best friend since childhood announced that she was engaged and asked if I*
> *would be her maid of honor. I was thrilled and excited and really looking forward*
> *to helping Vickie plan her wedding. The wedding was set for June, but they had been*
> *legally married in late August of the previous year for health insurance purposes.*
> *For reasons she never fully explained to me, her parents were not supposed to know.*
>
> *Fast-forward to right before the wedding. The preacher is refusing to per-*
> *form the ceremony unless someone can produce a marriage license. Well, since*
> *they were married months earlier, the license was already filed and the only*
> *copy was in the groom's dresser drawer. So I sent the groom home to get the li-*
> *cense and spent the time until he came back trying to calm the now-hysterical*
> *Vickie in the bathroom. Forty-five minutes later the groom returned and the*
> *wedding started. It went off without a hitch.*

Shame, shame, and eternal shame on that preacher for performing
a sham wedding ceremony. He didn't marry them; he participated in a
lie of the bride and groom's devising. They were lying to God by
speaking vows that had already been taken, lying to family and guests
who thought they were witnessing a first-time wedding ceremony, lying to each other that it was okay to inflict this type of deception on
their loved ones. Hiding the fact that a wedding has already occurred
was a dead giveaway that the bride and groom knew this was wrong.

You get only one shot at a wedding ceremony and if you choose to
use it with an informal visit to the justice of the peace, then that's
your wedding ceremony. You can't later decide to have the big wedding
of your dreams that dupes family and guests into believing you are
getting married for the first time and are deserving of all the perks associated with a large wedding.

Rule 13: When Mistakes Happen, We Are Calm, Cool, and Civil!

When my daughter's wedding day arrived, it was a record-breaking hot day in early June. Things were a little more hectic that morning, but amazingly, we arrived at the church a few minutes earlier than we had planned. While I was waiting in the back of our un-air-conditioned *church, the best man approached me and asked me for the groom's wedding band. I gave him a blank look. My daughter had told him that she had handed the ring to me. I thought back and remembered the bride handing me the pillow, a box for the pillow, and several papers through the window of the limo but no ring! Frantically, I went out to our car and looked through the trunk, seats, but no ring. One of my other daughter's friends kindly offered to run back to the house, a few blocks away, to see if I had dropped the box anywhere. She called on her cell phone to tell us "no ring."*

Now we were getting close to two o'clock, "start time." Stress levels were rising. I dumped my purse on a table and looked. No ring. Sweat was trickling down my back. Five minutes past two, my sister came to the back of the church to see what was wrong. As soon as she heard, being the levelheaded person is, she turned to my husband (who was like a deer in the headlights all day, with the thought of his "little girl" getting married and being very sentimental) and said to him, "Give me your hand!" *Having no idea what she was doing, but knowing better than to ask, he gave her his hand. She took hold of his wedding band and pulled it off. This ring had not left his hand for the past twenty-six years, so she really had to yank. She then handed the ring to the best man and said,* "Let's go!"

My son escorted me in, the music began, and the wedding ceremony went beautifully. No one else besides me, my husband, my sister, the best man, and of course, the happy couple knew that the wedding band being placed on our son-in-law's finger was my husband's. It fit perfectly! My daughter and I shared a few memorable winks and smiles throughout the ceremony. Later, at the reception, when the couple exited the limo, lo and behold, what should turn up stuck between the seats? The ring box! They had the groom's "real" ring blessed by the priest and now we have a great story to tell the grandkids!

Mistakes will happen even with the best of planning. With so many details to coordinate and people to direct, the odds are significant that there will be some glitch. If you approach the day expecting perfection, you will be disappointed, and that attitude will shine forth from your countenance for all to see. If, however, you have a realistic expectation that something could happen, you will be better prepared to cope with the inevitable. Have fun! Some mistakes become the fodder for family folklore.

Brideweena's Checklist

1. Have I contacted all the musicians and singers with my selections at least two months in advance of my wedding?

2. Do the officiant, photographer, videographer, DJ/band, florist, and baker know of the time and date of the wedding?

3. Have I remembered to take big deep breaths and not scream, scream, scream?

4. Have I corresponded with the church lady about the building's wedding policies?

5. Have the photographer and videographer been informed of any church policies that would restrict their movement?

6. Do I have enough seats for my guests?

7. Did I get the marriage license in advance?

8. Will the air-conditioning be turned on for my wedding?

9. Do the readers have their readings and know when they are to speak?

10. Have I written my vows?

11. Have I coached the flowergirl/ringbearer on what to expect?

12. Have I arranged for my honor attendant to hold the rings and the marriage license until the ceremony?

SEVEN

Wedding Receptions

That's the secret of entertaining. You make your guests feel welcome
and at home. If you do that honestly, the rest takes care of itself.
—BARBARA HALL

WITH THE PLANS FOR THE SERIOUS stuff behind you, it's
time to turn your attention to the party after the ceremony. If you thought there was already plenty of potential to offend your parents or the wedding attendants, just wait until
you plan the reception.

Contrary to legend, the reception is not for the bride and groom
but rather for the guests. You have invited them to witness a momentous event in your life and you have an obligation to entertain them.
Nearly every decision should be made with consideration for what
would be the gracious and hospitable choice for the guests. These people *are* your family and closest friends, are they not?

Hospitality is a two-edged sword. Hosts should provide for their
guests to the best of their financial ability (preferably without going
into debt) and guests should gratefully accept that hospitality without
expectation of being given more than the host can afford. That delicate balance between graciousness and gratitude can be upset by a

guest with unrealistic or presumptuous expectations or by a host who ignores the basic needs of her guests.

Guest hospitality should not be viewed as bending over backward attempting to fulfill unrealistic expectations of guests. Just as there are Bridezillas, there are guestzillas. Both groups have had the same twisted root of self-preoccupation and self-gratification blossom into expectations of what they believe is owed to them. Guestzillas will insist that any wedding worth attending will have copious quantities of alcohol, a sit-down dinner or live band, or some combination thereof. Some look down their noses at buffet dinners as a grave insult to their delicate sensibilities. Being a good host to one's guests does not obligate you to sacrifice your firstborn child for people with insatiable appetites or extravagant tastes. Ignore these people.

There are several recurrent themes throughout this chapter involving the appropriate decorum for a wedding reception. Considerate treatment of guests tops the list regarding appropriate decorum for a wedding reception. We also address issues relating to out-of-control or unseemly behavior and other potential pitfalls of partying too vigorously. We want to have fun, just not be ridiculous when we do. In this day of high-tech toys, the odds are quite good that several guests will have digital cameras or camera phones. Some people aren't above posting embarrassing photos on the Internet or wagging them in your teenagers' faces twenty years later. This is the start of your life together; it shouldn't be the start of your embarrassments together.

The Wedding Consultation

Brideweena: Aunt Fifi is insisting that I have to go all out with the reception to compensate guests for the generous gifts they will give us.

Miss Jeanne: Does Aunt Fifi have some preternatural ability to predict the amount of money guests will spend on gifts? It's not polite to presume to know what your wedding guests may choose to give as a wedding present. Come to think of it, engaged couples shouldn't even have an expectation of receiving wedding gifts lest it blossom into a full-blown sense of entitlement.

Brideweena: Aunt Fifi keeps asking what we're spending on the reception and how much my dress or the flowers cost.

Miss Jeanne: First, you are under no obligation to tell people what you are spending on the reception or any part of the wedding, for that matter. It's none of their business how much you spend, and polite people would never ask that question. Just smile enigmatically when she asks next time and then cheerfully change the subject to a discussion of the merits of NASCAR.

Brideweena: But Aunt Fifi will try to total up what she thinks we spent, and what if all my guests do that and resent that my reception was not equivalent to the cost of their wedding gift?

Miss Jeanne: I sincerely hope for your sake that you are not endowed with a passel of relations and acquaintances who harbor such petty attitudes. Guests should not be calculating what they plan to spend on a wedding gift based on what they think will be spent on the reception. Gifts are not the admission price to the reception. Brideweena, plan a reception that reflects your budget, your style and taste, and is appropriate for the time of day and you'll be fine.

Brideweena: Oh, Miss Jeanne, you are a rock of strength in the midst of my wedding maelstrom! What would I have done without you?

Miss Jeanne (muttering to herself): Probably had a wedding that was a repeat of Muffin Louise's travesty of presumptions, greed, and relational devastation.

Rule 1: Have the Proper Venue for the Guests

The very first decision you will make regarding the reception is where you would like to hold this party. At the head of your list of priorities for what constitutes an acceptable venue is how comfortable it will be for your guests. It always amazes me that some people can't think ahead to consider the consequences of packing 125 guests into an un-air-conditioned reception location in the dead of August in south Florida.

The second major factor is size. Does this site accommodate all the guests you wish to have at your wedding? You face a dilemma if the reception location will not accommodate the number of guests you originally had intended to invite. The choice before you is whether a stunningly beautiful reception location is more important than including everyone you want at your wedding.

Poor planning and lack of forethought result in receptions like this one:

Then, the reception. Or the death march where a reception should have been. We were herded into the church's "hall," which doubled as part of the preschool. No one had bothered to decorate, period, or bring in "big people" chairs. Not even streamers. We were surrounded by fingerpaintings, the room smelled like paste, and some of the fluorescent lights were flickering while making hissing and popping sounds. And there was nowhere to sit because there were only three or four full-sized seats for fifty guests. No tables either.

We all stood there staring at each other for an hour while the pictures were being taken. No one, even in the families, seemed to know each other. It was all but silent. I am absolutely positive that in the "six months of arduous planning" it never occurred to anyone that the guests would be waiting while they took pictures. They came back. Out came the grocery-store sheet cake: blank. Something to drink? Nothing. Not even pop or punch. I broke into the adjoining kitchen for tap water.

I've witnessed receptions like this and people routinely write to Etiquette Hell to complain about them. I'm not sure what the bride and groom were thinking, herding people like docile cattle into a feedlot, while they burn time on photography. The priorities are a bit skewed here. You need to walk through a reception location viewing it from a guest's perspective and asking yourself, "If I were a guest, would I enjoy myself?"

At this point we realized that there was nowhere for us to sit—and a fair amount of people were milling around in similar circumstances. I found a close friend of mine, a member of the bridal party, who confirmed to me that there were indeed about a hundred fewer seats than there were guests at the reception. The idea was that as soon as those people at the front of the buffet line were done eating, they were to relinquish their seats to those who were just making it to the food! Frustrated, hot, and starving, my fiancé and I politely chatted with other guests and the bridal party and waited for an acceptable time to make our exit.

Some people have this warped idea that providing fewer seats than guests in attendance will promote mingling among the guests. It doesn't. What it does promote is a competitive version of musical chairs where those who have one of the rare commodities are loath to leave it lest it get snatched up by the wandering chairless. It's survival of the fastest to park their rump roasts in the few chairs available.

Another consideration is whether the reception location would require significant cosmetic overhauling to transform it into a suitable wedding reception location.

To cut costs, since they were paying for this themselves, Lindsey and Troy did the cheapest thing I have ever been a witness to or been part of. Lindsey wanted to have a big wedding, but this is hard to do on no budget. So she figured she would just invite a bunch of people and hopefully they would come. She felt she needed a large place to accommodate all the people, but didn't want to rent a restaurant or hall because it was too expensive. We come from a town in northern Michigan, so what did she do? She contacted the people who own the indoor hockey rink where our high school and alumni hockey games are held. It is huge . . . like a football field indoors with a big concrete floor. During the summer . . . nothing is going on there anyway, so they rent it out to sporting events, on the rare occasions they do come along.

The people at the hockey rink said she would have the whole place for a hundred bucks . . . but that was too expensive for Lindsey and Troy. So Lindsey made a deal with them. The indoor hockey rink was housing the Shrine Circus the day before the wedding. If she could find someone to clean up after the circus left, she could have the place for fifty bucks. So she volunteers the wedding party to clean up after the Shrine Circus so she can save fifty bucks. We had to meet at the indoor rink at nine P.M. after the last circus show with brooms and cleaning supplies. I had no idea what we were in for.

Firstly, the circus had just finished, so they needed time to remove all of their equipment, animals, and whatnot. The last rack of cotton candy didn't go out of that place until eleven thirty P.M. We had to sit there and wait. When everyone was cleared out . . . there was so much work to be done. Not only were the bleachers full of garbage, but there was animal feces everywhere. Elephant poop, tiger poop . . . poop everywhere! Lindey and Troy had to run out and spend like more than a hundred bucks buying shovels, disinfectant, buckets, trash cans, and trash bags. Many of us were gagging cleaning up the runny feces from the ground . . . it was terrible.

Not only were we supposed to clean this up and make it smell "unlike a barnyard" (whatever!) but she brought a bunch of decorations. Which she insisted on putting up. They looked ridiculous. The largest "fold-out" bell could not compete with the huge open space and the gray dismal nature of a huge indoor hockey rink large enough to host the Shrine Circus. We were there cleaning up poop and straw and hanging up decorations, which looked invisible in the concrete vastness of the rink, until three A.M. We had to be at Troy's house for the outdoor wedding by ten A.M., over an hour's drive away. I was actually brutally tired, having worked all day that day, and I asked Lindsey if she would mind if I went home at about one A.M. She just got really angry and said, "Whatever!" and stormed off to whisper about me to Troy. I was not sure if I would be able to get up and be presentable the following morning, but I stayed on, pushing my poop-crusted broom across the entire length of the rink . . . I swear that each pass felt like it took a day from my life. . . .

This certainly qualifies as a "torture the attendants" story that is mitigated only by the fact that the bride and groom are joining right in with the misery. If you have to do a major face-lift to a site to get it reception-ready using all volunteer help, think long and hard before signing the contract to rent the place. Volunteer labor should be budgeted just like money. If you don't have commitments of help in the "bank," you should never presume that you can obtain that labor at a later date.

Immutable Fact of Life

If your volunteers have put in more than four hours decorating or preparing the ceremony or reception location the day before, you need to provide them with a meal. Otherwise, that grumbling you will hear may not be empty stomachs.

Rule 2: Mealtimes Require a Meal

Well, after spending $25,000 on a dress, tuxes, flowers, and a photographer, they couldn't afford food. They served cake and punch at the reception that lasted from five P.M. to seven P.M. They expected people to eat before or after the reception.

The rules that matter with regard to food for a wedding reception are simple. If you invite people to join you in celebrating your wedding during a typical mealtime, you are obligated to serve that meal. Guests will conclude from the time of the wedding that a meal will be served. Not to do so is just plain cheap and cruel. If you want to know what people will be muttering behind your backs, read on. . . .

With our drinks we made our way to the only seats available, which were in front of the speakers. The music was so loud that it was deafening. The other guests informed us that the bridal party hadn't taken any photos before the cer-

emony, and that we were waiting on the photography session. This was just after six P.M., and we were expected to sit there drinking alcohol on empty stomachs until the bridal party arrived. No snacks, no appetizers, nothing. Fortunately, no one got drunk on their empty stomachs during the wait—most people sat quietly at their tables, nursing one of those expensive drinks. Some of the children were running around, but even they quieted down eventually. I plastered my biggest smile on my face and made polite conversation with several scowling faces. We had no idea how long things were supposed to take, so when they finally arrived at eight P.M., everyone was eager to get things started.

Finally, they went through the food lines. I managed to get in line about three quarters of the way back. The lines were going very slowly. It took about forty-five minutes for me to get close enough to even see what the food was. Once I did, I noticed people's faces more than the food. They were disgusted, and I heard several comments along the lines of "That's it?" and "Can you believe this?" That's when I noticed that the food was only appetizers.

Schedule your wedding during a lunch or dinner hour and then tantalize your guests with barely enough food and you have a recipe for ravenous guests. They are armed and dangerous and know how to type a scathing e-mail to www.etiquettehell.com to complain about your inhospitable reception.

That's not to say that cake and punch receptions are tacky or some kind of heinous faux pas. Far from it! Guestzillas will try to guilt-manipulate you with dire warnings of guest revulsion but they are grossly mistaken. If you cannot afford more than cake and punch or desire to serve hors d'oeuvres, then schedule your reception to occur between 1:30 and 4:30 P.M. or later in the evening after dinner.

I have read many terrible stories but nothing compares to the audacity of one of my coworkers. "Debbie" was getting married after she was reacquainted with her high school sweetheart and soon became engaged. We were all very happy and excited for her. The first surprise was the request that instead of gifts, the couple wanted the girls of the office (about twenty of us) to contribute to the reception. A sign-up list was put on the wall.

One word about potlucks: don't. If you can't afford the wedding reception of your dreams, it is beyond tacky to corral the guests into being caterers. I've had people attempt to justify obligatory potluck wedding receptions—in which guests are asked to bring a dish or even assigned dishes to bring—by claiming it is their cultural heritage. The problems with that are (I) it would be presumptuous to assume all your guests are of the same cultural heritage and wouldn't mind being depended upon to cater the reception, and (2) just because your ancestors may have been rude, cheeky boors does not mean you have to carry on the tradition.

It is perfectly fine if family or friends take the initiative to volunteer to prepare and bring food for a wedding reception. I've done it many times. The faux pas occurs when such generosity is expected as an obligation or something that can be demanded, rather than a voluntary offer of generosity to be received with gratitude.

Rule 3: Food, Glorious Food!

If do you choose to feed your guests a meal, be prepared to compromise on the menu.

Next error was in planning her reception—a ten-course Chinese banquet. Even though she knew several of her guests are vegetarians, every single dish she selected was a meat or seafood dish. During the planning stages I suggested she should have at least one vegetable dish to accommodate those guests who do not eat meat. She said, "Oh, it's okay, they are all served on vegetables." Now, I know some vegetarians who are so strict they won't even eat something that has been on the same plate as a meat or egg dish, let alone veggies that have been sitting under the meat! In any case, the food was served on veggies—if you can consider a lettuce garnish a veggie! After the third nonvegetarian dish was served, the spouse of a vegetarian at my table asked the waiter to please have the cook make up some chow mein so his wife could have something to eat. In the meantime, she was trying to be a good sport, picking out bits of broccoli and carrots from the serving plates so she didn't starve. She even tried a bit of what we all thought were some sort of clear noodles, but which none of us liked, very rubbery. Imagine her horror later when the bride told us it was jellyfish!

You can't possibly cater to every food preference guests may have but your menu choices should have enough variety to satisfy most of them. If you know there are vegetarians on your guest list, at least try to accommodate that preference. Barring food allergies, people who get their shorts in a wad because they can't have prime rib instead of chicken should be ignored.

After a lovely but hot ceremony, the pastor announced that we were all invited to the reception. This was also being held outside on the church grounds, and that we should "all help ourselves to the food" because there's "lots and lots, and we don't want any of it to be wasted." Okay, fine. My fiancé and I were starving, because it was now around seven in the evening, and we hadn't yet eaten anything. However, because of our spots in the seating arrangement at the ceremony, we were the very last to make it through the receiving line and get to the buffet of food. It was at this point that we found that there was practically nothing left to eat—since there obviously wasn't all that much to begin with. All that was left was a few scraps of fruit and veggies, and some finger sandwiches—containing tuna, eggs, and mayo—that had been left out in the Southern heat for the entirety of the ceremony and reception! My fiancé and I declined to partake of what was left of the food.

Do-it-yourself catering or nonprofessional catering is great! I wholeheartedly support these types of receptions. They have two potential drawbacks that you should be prepared to address, however. First is food service safety. You don't want your wedding remembered as the one in which a quarter of the guests were two-stepping it with great alacrity to commune with the porcelain throne. Church receptions are notorious for food that is not stored or served at proper temperatures. Hot dishes should be kept at 140 degrees minimum and cold dishes under 40 degrees. Buy a ten-dollar food service temperature probe for the servers at your reception. Second, serve enough food for all the guests. There is nothing worse than running out of food before the line has gone through the buffet.

Rule 4: It's Not a Fund-Raiser

They first had a money dance where you pin money to the bride's dress to dance with her. Then they had some bizarre game where the bride is "kidnapped" and you have to pay a ransom for her. I escaped from the disaster as soon as I was able.

Just how many cutesy "games" and schemes can be devised to separate guests from as much of their cash as possible? Quite a few, apparently—everything from the increasingly ubiquitous money dance to bizarre drinking games or outright selling of the center-pieces. I've even heard of the bride and groom selling wedding cook-ies at $20 apiece—weddings as bake sales! What a novel idea! Not. Weddings are not to be excuses for fund-raising regardless of what your friends and mother may tell you.

Money dancing, in particular, is a gross distor-tion of a once-common courtesy the bride and groom were expected to show their guests. If you have dancing at your wedding reception, you have an obligation to dance with anyone who requests the pleasure. The courtesy of dancing with one's  guests is just that, a courtesy. Money dancing takes this gracious cour-tesy the guests of honor are to bestow on their guests freely and cheapens it into a business transaction wherein guests must now pay for something that etiquette demanded was owed to whoever asked for the favor of a dance.

The root of the motivation for this "tradition" becomes evident when money is removed from the equation. Is the reason to do a money dance to spend time with guests and offer them a dance with the bride or groom? Then alternative methods of "paying" for that dance would be employed, such as providing little note cards and pen-cils for guests to write a blessing for the couple which then becomes the "admission price" of a dance while someone reads the blessing during each dance. It achieves the objective of spending time with in-dividual guests without cheapening the courtesy of dancing with those who desire to.

Or is the reason to do a money dance to acquire more cash from guests? For those who insist their families expect it and will not be as generous unless there is a money dance, do you really want to twirl around the dance floor as a prerequisite for someone's gift? It's a gift with strings attached, and people degrade themselves to being nothing more than performers who expect to be paid well for their performance. Some people don't hide their expectant glee at how much money they stand to rake in from a money dance. People like this brazenly expose the real reason behind a money dance: it's another cash cow. Like rancid milk, it leaves a sour taste in the mouths of those expected to spread that wallet open as wide as it can go.

Rule 5: Smashed to Pieces

There's questionable cake smashing . . .

The ceremony went off without a hitch, but then the reception began and all hell broke loose. The entire wedding party, made up of the bride and groom's friends, and their girlfriends, proceeded to get extremely drunk. During the cake cutting, the bride and groom smeared the cake all over each other (not just their faces) and then the wedding party started throwing cake everywhere. This was inside the house, and cake was smashed into the white carpet, on the walls, on the curtains—you name it, it had cake on it. My boyfriend and I were appalled, as were the other adults at the party. We helped clean everything up, much to the gratification of the bride's parents and the other older people. We were the only young people there who were not behaving like animals.

And then there's assault by wedding cake ...

About twelve years ago I was a bartender for a wedding reception of a young couple in an upscale catering facility in northwest New Jersey. This is an area that still has many country folks living among the transplanted yuppies from the New York metropolitan area. As the afternoon wore on, I suggested to the groom that he not have any more beer since he had consumed quite a bit and the dinner was still in progress. He informed me that "I don't haf to worry none, we got a limo to drive us." Although I cut him off, he succeeded in getting friends to obtain beer for him. When it came time to cut the cake, the guests gathered around the three-tiered wedding cake that was on a pedestal table. The bride took a bit of the cake and smeared it lovingly on the groom's nose and mouth. The groom proceeded to put his right arm around the bride's neck in a headlock and pushed her face down into the cake. The bride grasped the edges of the table to lift her face out of the cake. The table tipped over, the cake fell to the floor, and the couple fell into the cake. The videographer was hovering over them as this occurred. There was total silence. The bride and her mother ran to the ladies' room muttering obscenities, cleaned up, and then left. I don't know what happened after that.

Do you have food fights in restaurants you two frequent? Do you typically fling food at each other at family get-togethers? No? I didn't think so. So why would you engage in juvenile food play at your wedding reception?

Feeding each other a taste of cake is meant to symbolize the beginning of a life of shared nurturing of each other. What symbolic interpretation do you think people come away with after witnessing a cake smash, regardless of whether it was meant in fun?

Men who shove their bride facefirst into the wedding cake have serious abuse issues and it's no mystery why the bride's male family members have then introduced the groom to that family delicacy known as a knuckle sandwich. While I would hope aggressive cake smashing would not dissolve into a familial slugfest, I do think it portends misfortune for the marriage, and serious consideration should be given as to whether the marriage should be annulled right then and there. Why marry a man willing to ruin your expensive clothing and destroy a costly dessert all for the pleasure of humiliating you in public? If your groom chides you about being a "good sport" about this prospect, ask him—and yourself—what other degradations he'll expect you to be a "good sport" about once you are married to him.

Rule 6: The Waiting Game

The time between the ceremony and the reception is fast becoming the most abused portion of the wedding day. The variety of ways to inconvenience guests is staggering in its creativity!

The reception was at a VFW hall about fifteen minutes' drive from the church. The hall has a bar area toward the front and a meeting hall in the back, where the reception was held. I want to make clear that I'm not complaining about the setting for the reception. They used folding tables and chairs but there were nice tablecloths and pretty decorations, and good hearty food cooking in the kitchen. The wedding party wasn't there yet when we arrived, but people had fun talking with relatives.

After an hour of waiting for the wedding party, we were starting to get antsy, not to mention hungry. The food was ready, but of course it wouldn't be served until the bride and groom were there. I managed to discreetly grab some carrot sticks and a roll. We were wondering how long before the meal would be served, when I noticed one of the groomsmen enter near the back of the hall. He didn't stick around long, but I figured the reception would be starting soon. No such luck. Half an hour later my girlfriend's mother and I decided to go to the bar and get some beer. What do we discover but the entire wedding party in the bar watching a college football game! Worse yet, it was only the third quarter!

The bride and groom finally graced us with their presence about two and a half hours after the reception was supposed to start. There was going to be music and possibly dancing afterward, but it was late by then and many of the cousins with young children were heading home. We left with them.

It's bad enough to keep guests on tenterhooks and hungry while the wedding photography finishes. It's even worse when the delay is due to a college basketball or football game. People would be surprised at how many stories I get of this nature where the bridal party or the groom and his attendants have evacuated themselves from the reception to watch a game on the hotel sports bar television or on a small TV someone brought. The football game was more important than gracing the guests with their presence and commencing the official start of the reception.

I have recently been witness to one of the most appalling wedding "traditions." We went to a wedding in a small town an hour away, and the invitation stated that there would be a dinner reception immediately following the ceremony. The ceremony was very nice . . . at a historic church, lots of music, and very formal.

We went to the reception at a local hotel. And then waited, and waited, and waited. It took the bride and groom an hour and a half to appear at the reception (and hence for the 150-plus guests to be served dinner). Everyone was generally irritated, but none complained as we didn't want to upset the bride and groom.

A few weeks after the wedding, my husband told me the reason the bride and groom took so long getting to the reception. It was because of a "tradition" in this small town where the wedding party takes the bride and groom to a strip club immediately after the wedding ceremony. There are no words to express my utter disgust at this "tradition."

I have been getting more and more stories of similar escapades by newlyweds and their bridal parties immediately following the ceremony. Barhopping, strip-club jaunts, riding around town in the limo and getting drunk, photography shoots at numerous different locations, even full sit-down meals while guests cool their jets at the reception site waiting for the guests of honor to arrive. If a couple would have such disdain for their guests as to treat them in this fashion, why bother inviting them at all? The answer is that the guests have really been used as a means to get more bridal booty, and once that has been obtained, how they get treated is of little importance. After all, they have served their function as giftbearers, so now they can get lost.

A less egregious but nonetheless annoying delay between the ceremony and reception would be . . .

Wedding starts at two P.M. Betsy is radiant in her huge gown, groom Shawn is beaming, and we proceed through the ceremony, complete with full Mass. Gets so hot in the church, the bride and groom have to sit down to avoid overheating. Wedding is over at about three thirty, bride and groom are whisked away to the luncheon at a local hotel. We are invited to this, so we attend, have a light sandwich and salad lunch, eat wedding cake, and after the meal is over, there is a three-hour lull in the festivities until the dance starts at eight P.M. My husband and I go home for a while, and return at eight.

What exactly were the out-of-town guests or those who invested some time in driving to the wedding to do during that three-hour gap between the luncheon reception and the dance? Hang out at the local McDonald's, twiddling their thumbs waiting? That question may sound facetious but I have an actual copy of a wedding invitation insert a storyteller sent me in which the bride does advise her guests that the local McDonald's restaurant is a suitable place to kill those three hours before the reception starts. As we can see from the other stories, guests are not above calling it quits and leaving a reception or simply not attending if their goodwill has been abused. If you have to have a long gap between ceremony and reception activities, at the bare minimum you should provide a hospitality room for guests to relax in, or perhaps a relative can have an open house during that lull in activities.

Rule 7: Cash Bars

Whether to have a cash bar or not is a source of great dissension. Some people view it as necessary to cater to guests who are of the belief they will wither and die if they can't have alcohol at a wedding regardless of whether the bride and groom can afford it. On the other hand, cash bars can be a weasely way of avoiding higher catering bills by passing on the expense to the guests. The Etiquette Hell perspective is that it is terribly rude to compel your wedding guests to open their wallets for anything. They are your guests. Treat them so.

My husband and I were invited with my family to my cousin's wedding in a town about three hours away. More than half of the guests had to travel at least one hour so many of us were staying in the hotel where the reception was held. We were quite excited. We all arrived at the church and my husband leaned over and mentioned that apparently it was going to be a cash bar. I assumed he was joking and laughed but he insisted. He and a couple of other cousins finally convinced me and I was shocked. I realize that cash bars are becoming more common but I think it's only fair at least to warn people ahead of time so they can come prepared. Since most of us were from out of town, it was a scramble from the church to the reception to try to find a bank in a strange town.

The ultimate convenience to guests would have been to install an automatic cash machine in the reception foyer so they can get the cash to pay for the drinks the hosts should have provided for free. Just give it time and some cretin will come up with this brilliant idea as a justifiable excuse for providing a convenient method for guests to divest themselves of their cash.

But just when you think it can't possibly get worse, someone ups the ante to the heights of rudeness....

From there, we proceeded to the bar, and some guests approached the food stations. The MC barked loudly at them, "The food stations are closed until the bridal party goes through first." I was surprised at that, but then I noticed everyone else was sitting down at the tables with drinks only. I shrugged it off, and asked my husband to get me a drink. He asked which one, to which I said, "Whatever, I don't care." He then pointed out that we had to buy tickets at another station first; the bar was accepting only tickets for drinks. I was really puzzled, but we went to the ticket station anyway. My chin nearly hit the floor when I saw the sign posted on the table. Not only was it a cash bar for alcohol—but sodas, juice, and bottled water were more expensive than wine or beer, which were at hotel premium prices.

There were children running around demanding that aunts and uncles buy them a soda. I couldn't believe it. I was so startled that I requested tap water.

My husband was getting really impatient that I wouldn't make up my mind, because, you see, they didn't offer tap water. The bar was instructed that all water served must be sold with a ticket. Fortunately, he had brought cash, otherwise we would have had nothing to drink all night.

Making guests pay for *water* is so evil, it defies comprehension. It is the ultimate expression of tasteless, cheap, crass, inhospitable entertaining. Pull this stunt and your guests will make a mental portrait of you for inclusion in their tacky hall of shame. In it they will throw a few imaginary fiery darts at you on occasion, while never uttering a peep to you about what a hosting ogre you have been.

Rule 8: You Don't Have to Have Alcohol

In the receiving line, one guest introduced me to her date who said only one thing to me, "What kind of beer are you serving?" When I told them that I wasn't serving alcohol (it was an afternoon reception) he rolled his eyes and walked away from me without ever saying anything to my brand-spanking-new husband. At the reception I went over to be polite and talk to her and she told me, so a lot of people could hear, that it was dumb of me not to have alcohol because people would be bored.

I have to admit that this kind of guest irks me to no end. They aren't interested in congratulating you on this entry to a new stage of life but only in how they can be personally gratified. They are the ones most likely to defy an alcohol ban that your reception site has and sneak in the booze.

You are under no legal or etiquette obligation to serve alcohol in any form to your guests. There are plenty of excellent reasons not to serve alcohol at a wedding reception, including religious observances, budgetary constraints, a desire not to tempt the family alcoholics. If people are bored because there is no alcohol to lubricate their pleasure senses, this says more about the quality of their character than about the quality of your hospitality.

There are, in fact, some serious issues of legal liability if you serve alcohol:

The day of the wedding my sister-in-law had rented a very nice new bus to transport her wedding party and their dates. The wedding party made sure that this bus was very well stocked with coolers of beer. I must admit I was a bit peeved when the wedding party was using expletives to describe my mother, who insisted on no drinking before the ceremony. Perhaps I was again a bit sensitive when I saw the twelve- and thirteen-year-old ushers getting drunk off the provided beer, and yet again when, during the reception, I was going down the table with a bottle of champagne refilling glasses and I caught heat for not giving some to the very underage ushers.

If you are planning on serving alcohol at your wedding reception, it is crucial that you be aware of your legal responsibilities as the host. You can bear the legal burden if you serve alcohol to intoxicated guests who later injure themselves or injure or kill someone else. According to the law, you are responsible for your guests even if the event is a wedding hosted by a private individual. As if that were not enough of a legal obligation, hosts of the party are equally responsible for their guests until they are sober. Allow your guests to get plastered and you will have upped your legal liability potential considerably.

Serving alcohol to minors is illegal in many states, and if he or she is found to be negligent in restricting alcohol, the host will bear the entire legal responsibility. Extricating yourself from criminal and civil lawsuits is not the way to start off a marriage.

The Wedding Consultation

Brideweena: Since we can't afford champagne for all our guests, will we rot in Etiquette Hell if we serve champagne to the bridal party only and let guests toast with water?

Miss Jeanne: Yes . . . you'll not only rot but stink too. It's just not polite to serve different food and beverages to one set of guests, even if they are the bridal party, and something else to another subset of guests. *Très* rude!

Curtis: I guess this means I don't get to have prime rib for my reception dinner, right? I thought everyone else would be happy with chicken.

Miss Jeanne: I think you'll survive the deprivation for one night.

Rule 9: Some Decorum, Please!

Hmm, didn't we cover this topic in another chapter? It bears repeating: Just because it is your wedding day and everyone is here to party hearty in your honor, you really don't want to brand memories of an out-of-control bridal brat in people's minds.

The final minutes of the reception concluded with shrieking from upstairs. The bride had finally stopped pretending to be mad at the groom in regard to the bachelor party incident. Everyone remaining at the reception was treated to a screaming match between the bride and groom. Finally, they came downstairs in their departure clothes with some very obvious fake smiles and left in their limo. The rest of us had another drink.

The bride and groom divorced a year later.

Gosh, couldn't that have waited until they were at least in the getaway car and a mile down the road?

All was going well and the guests were enjoying themselves when it came time for the toasts. The best man, the groom's brother, was very nervous and making a valiant effort at his speech, which he almost pulled off. I say almost, because at the end he wished all the best to his brother and . . . the girl who the groom had been engaged to previously and who had cheated on him and run off. Shock followed but the bride did not let anyone compose themselves long enough to feel sorry for her before she stood up, pointing at the offending speaker, and screamed a vile curse at him. Really classy girl. Needless to say, the dining room was barren fifteen minutes later.

This is an excellent example of how the behavior of the bride or groom can affect the atmosphere of the reception profoundly. Incidents may happen but how you respond to them will be a testimony to your graciousness, or lack of it. No matter how irritated you are, no matter how egregious the offense is, no matter that the perpetrator is deserving of getting his nincompoop face smacked off, all eyes will be on you on your wedding day. You don't need to scream at people, stomp around the reception in high dudgeon, or flip the bird and curse.

If you can't hold your liquor well, consider imbibing in moderation or not at all. Most ridiculous behavior occurs due to more alcohol consumption than is prudent. You might have a good chance of remembering to be civil while sober, but lubricate the mouth and disconnect the brain with too much alcohol, and you decrease the odds of behaving kindly to people. Excessive alcohol can impair your sense of decorum as well. Do you really want to be remembered for stripping yourself naked and yodeling a hearty Tarzan jungle call before diving off the hotel balcony into the hotel swimming pool? And oh! The photos your guests will take to use for blackmail purposes later!

My entire family was invited to a cousin's wedding. My dad RSVP'd that he would be attending, but his golf tournament went over and he was winning and couldn't leave. My sister decided to bring her sixteen-year-old daughter in my dad's place. She did it with the best of intentions—so that my cousin would not have to pay for an unused plate. Besides, my niece is a very quiet, shy girl (read: not loud or any trouble) and not a stranger to my cousin. Plus, my niece actually wanted to go—she was excited.

I arrived later into cocktail hour and my sister came up to me saying she was leaving. I asked why. My cousin (the bride) had seen my sister standing in line at the bar and went to say hello. Her jaw had dropped when she saw my niece. She said, "What is she doing here? I don't have room for her! She should leave!" My sister, shocked at the outburst, said, "My father can't make it because his tournament ran over. I brought Nicole in his place so you wouldn't have to pay for an uneaten dinner." The bride then repeated her three phrases: "What is she doing here? I don't have room for her! She should leave!" My sister replied calmly, "You do have room, she is taking my father's place because he cannot make it. My father was supposed to be seated at my table." The bride again repeated herself: "What is she doing here? I don't have room for her! She should

leave!" Then, a woman, unknown to my sister, came up to the bride and said,
"It's okay. You have the room. Someone didn't show. It's okay." The bride then
walked off in a huff. Keep in mind, my niece heard this entire exchange.

Even if a guest presumes too much by inviting another guest, your
response should not be one of berating like a harpy. Calmness should
prevail; it will be okay.

Immutable Fact of Life

Everyone is either bored or offended by the stupid game of "return
the groom's apartment key." It always was a stupid game made more
stupid and boring over time as it gets played to death in wedding after wedding. It involves the best man asking all the ladies in the audience to return the groom's apartment keys now that he is a married
man. By prior arrangement, various young women come forward one
by one and drop keys in the best man's hand. Finally, he asks if there
is anyone else and either an elderly grandmother or a young girl or
man comes forward with the final key. Implying the groom is either
promiscuous, homosexual, incestuous, or into pedophilia is rude beyond measure. It is not particularly original anymore either.

Rule 10: To Receive or Not to Receive

The wedding was at two P.M. and seemed to go off without a hitch. Afterward,
guests milled about outside the church, but there was no receiving line. The re-
ception started at six P.M. across town. Our family was seated at two tables.
Food was good, activities standard. But the bride and groom did not circulate
among the guests! I heard later that the bride had said, more or less, This is my
night and I'll do as I please. The groom came to our table alone for a few min-

*utes. But the night ended, the happy couple left, and the bride had made no ef-
fort to meet any of the groom's family! I was stunned and appalled. Had I not
met her the day before, I would have been furious; as it was, I was upset in be-
half of my sister and cousins who hadn't had a chance to meet her previously.
I doubt I'll be making any effort in the future.*

Your obligation, both groom and bride, is to greet the guests. If
you do not do this by receiving line, you need to make a concerted effort to go from table to table greeting and thanking guests for coming. They have come at your family's invitation to honor and support
you. Standing in the corner like a pretty doll on display won't cut it. If
you haven't met some of your new in-laws before this point, for the
sake of family peace, it would be an especially good idea to press the
flesh.

*On to the reception, which meant you had to leave the church and get back on
the main highway (thirty miles or so) and then travel another forty miles to the
reception hall located, you guessed it, in the middle of nowhere. The reception
hall held 150 people, which meant thankfully everyone got a seat. However, we
were packed in there because the food table, cake table, and gift table took up the
majority of the space. The bridal party table was located on top of a stage of
sorts that gave the effect of the bride and groom towering over you and also
made it impossible to talk to them. The bride almost never left the stage because
the only set of stairs leading to it were very small and she almost tripped each
time she tried to navigate them.*

Be sure to make yourself available for guests to come and greet you
too. You shouldn't plan so many activities at the reception that you are
racing from one thing to another and it keeps you from socializing

with your guests. People will want to greet and congratulate you and they shouldn't have to chase you all over the reception site to do it. In fact, the inability to greet and congratulate the bride and groom ranks in the top ten of pet peeves people have about weddings, so make it a priority to greet as many guests as possible.

The Wedding Consultation

Miss Jeanne: We need to have a practice session on how to move along those chatty guests who can monopolize your time in the receiving line.

Curtis: Thank heavens! Uncle Frito can yammer on and on, totally oblivious to anyone or anything around him.

Miss Jeanne: It is important to greet each guest to the wedding reception, but the receiving line is not the time to catch up on the memories. Brideweena, after greeting the guest and thanking him for coming to share the day with you, put his hand into Curtis's hand and say, "Let me introduce to you my wonderful new husband, Curtis." As he greets him, turn sweetly away and greet your next guest in the receiving line. Uncle Frito will never know what hit him.

Rule 11: Appropriate Music, Please!

I am a DJ. I have been a DJ for about fifteen years, for parties and weddings, as well as five years on radio. A friend of mine, also a DJ, wound up in the hospital with a reception to do that weekend. He contacted me, and gave me the details (bride was twenty-four, groom was twenty-six, about ninety people at a particular lodge), then asked me to cover for him. I was available, and he of-

fered his equipment to supplement mine if needed. Turns out I didn't need it, but the offer was nice. He wanted to make sure his client was taken care of. I respect that.

I got in touch with the bride three days before the wedding, and informed her of the situation. I gave my credentials, and gave her the opportunity to ask any questions she might have. My friend also called her from the hospital to apologize, and recommended me to put her fears to rest. The bride seemed fine with the arrangement, we agreed to the same price she was paying my friend, which was just a little less than my usual fee, and he was going to forward the deposit to me. (I had just recently gotten married myself, and did not want to rip her off.) I got the information from her about the songs she wanted, when she wanted them, setup information, and all of the other things a professional DJ does.

I use a computer to play music the vast majority of the time. I had the songs she wanted on the hard drive. I always bring a CD player and CDs as backup. This one time I wish I hadn't.

At the appropriate time, the guests begin trickling in. I had light classical and smooth jazz playing as background music while people ate and waited for the wedding party. As requested. About an hour later I get the signal that the bride and groom have arrived. I make the announcement, and direct everyone's attention to the door. As requested. The bride and groom walk in, and make a quick swing around the room. Obviously smashed—both of them. I didn't think you could get that drunk in one hour. The bride reaches under her dress (!!) and pulls out a CD. She hands it to me and tells me to, "Play track three, I wanna paaaaaarrrrttttttaaaayyy!!! Woooooo!!!!!"

Oh, boy. I hadn't bargained for this. I stalled for a moment while I listened to track three in the headphones. Like I said, I've been doing this for fifteen years. I've heard quite a bit in that time, but this was the most profane, violently sexual, explicit, booty-shakin' rap song that ever managed to stick to a

CD. And I had never heard it before. It was on a blank CD, so I didn't even know who it was. I'm listening to this in the headphones, while I'm looking at her grandmother, sitting politely there with her purse in her lap, looking like the upstanding lady she probably is. I try to convince the bride that this may not be appropriate, especially considering there were children there.

All for naught. She said (loudly), "I will not pay you unless you play the song." This was even before any of the other traditional dances. I glanced at the father of the bride, who shrugged and nodded his head, as if to say, "Go ahead—just to shut her up." So I prefaced the song by announcing that it was a special request from the bride. And I pushed play.

The bride and groom were having a convulsion on the dance floor, I think. As soon as the lyrics started, jaws dropped. One mother covered her kids' ears. Literally. It must have taken a moment or two for Grandma to get the volume on her hearing aids right, but as soon as she started understanding the words, she stood up, grabbed her granddaughter, the bride, by the arm, and dragged her back to the DJ table. Grandma was screaming at her, "Tell him to turn it off!!" I stopped the music. Grandma yelled at me, "I didn't tell you to stop it, she is going to stop it. Put it back on!"

So I said, "Yes, ma'am!" and restarted it. The bride must have sobered up a little, because she begged me to stop it. The people in attendance were now rolling on the floor laughing. I stopped the song. By this time the father of the bride was up there, and I told him, "I hope you understand, but I would like to be paid now. In cash, please. I don't want any misunderstandings later." He pulled out his wallet, grinning. Grandma let go of her granddaughter, and stomped back to her seat. I announced, "Ladies and gentleman, the grandmother of the bride!" She got a well-deserved standing ovation. The festivities continued.

A plate of food and a couple cups of coffee later, the bride was apologetic. I accepted her apology, and she tipped me $100. After the reception, I asked the videographer if I could have a copy of the tape, to use as warning to people who want to get a little extreme with their music at a family function, and for lifting my spirits after a rough day. Turns out the father of the bride paid him extra for an unedited copy. He was going to show it to his daughter's children when their time came to get married.

I'm nearly always amazed at what music gets played at wedding receptions. What are people thinking when "The Way We Were" is used for the first dance? Umm, hello? The breakup song's lyrics may not set exactly the tone you had in mind, despite its flowing melody. Many people don't even really listen to the songs they select, until perhaps it is too late to repent of their sentimental selection of based on the pleasant melody or hoppin' rhythm.

The bride and groom were announced and entered the reception to AC/DC's "Highway to Hell."

Now was this a premonition of their married life or could it be that they had some foresight into their guests pitching them into Etiquette Hell?

Rule 12: Photography

The wedding ceremony itself went off okay, but then the reception started. Or rather, it didn't start. I'm used to the idea of waiting for the bride and groom to finish a photo shoot before attending the reception, and I know that can take forty-five minutes to an hour. But an hour came and went, we had only a cheese tray for nibbles (it was a lunchtime wedding, and a full lunch was to be served), and no one had any idea where they were, including the groom's parents, my in-laws. We then discovered that the bride, groom, bridesmaids, ushers, and bride's parents went to a nearby rose garden to have their pictures taken. Groom's parents? Not important enough, or too ugly, I guess, even if they did pay for half of the affair. In one fell swoop they've ticked off everyone: the groom's side of the family (including my husband) and the partygoers (who feel like they're being strung along). People start to leave (including us).

When the less-than-thoughtful bridal party arrives at the "banquet" an hour and a half after the wedding ceremony, they find less than forty people out of the original one hundred waiting for them.

If you think about it, the bride and groom typically have eyes only for each other at the moment she begins her processional. It's a magic moment for the two of them, but it's being shared with two hundred friends and family members too. After that, it's a whirlwind of activity, with the ceremony and then the reception passing by in a blur, and precious little time to be alone or soak up the uniqueness of the day.

With prewedding photography, the first time the groom sees the bride can be arranged in any of several different ways. The bride waits sequestered in a room by herself and the groom enters alone. Or the groom is standing at the front of the church while everyone else has removed themselves to give the couple some privacy and the bride processes into the sanctuary by herself. They then have time to savor the moment alone, to look at each other in detail and admire the dress and hairdos and flowers and tux, to pray together, to calm nerves, to have time to really focus together on what is about to occur. Many people have told me this was the most poignant, spiritual time of the entire day and no one has regretted it. It does not diminish the specialness of the bride's processional down the aisle at the actual wedding because what is important there is not what she looks like but rather the symbolism of the processional. It represents leaving one's parents or singlehood to embark on a new life joined with the other person. In Jewish weddings, the bride and groom see each other prior to the wedding ceremony as part of the Ketubah signing ceremony. There is nothing wrong with the groom's seeing the bride before the ceremony, especially if it will allow the reception then to proceed on a schedule that is kind to the guests. A nontraditional act of kindness might make a good start of a new tradition itself.

Prewedding photography can be so much more relaxing compared to the rush-rush from one pose to another as the photographer tries to get the maximum number of posed, formal shots into a limited time frame after the wedding ceremony. Attendants not required for specific shots can lounge contentedly in the church pews talking and enjoying the moment. The bride's makeup is not ruined with sweat and tears as everyone hurries and scurries through what should be a relaxed and enjoyable day.

Rule 13: Guests as Waitstaff

In order to save money, you may be tempted by the idea of using guests as your labor force. Don't.

I knew I wasn't a bridesmaid, and I was totally fine with that—I would have been shocked to have been asked. So when Tonya asked me ever so sweetly if I'd pour champagne at the wedding I was touched. Of course I'd be happy to pour champagne. I thought it was a kind way to include me in the wedding.

Well, after the ceremony I went to the reception area and there was a buffet set up, rather formal and very nice. Suddenly, though, I was grabbed by the wedding coordinator who asked if I was Hillary, the one in charge of drinks. I was a little taken aback at going from pouring champagne to being "in charge of drinks," but I said that I was. The woman took me to a table, with boxes of liquor and boxes of napkins, lemons, and glasses behind it. Apparently, I was the bartender. I started setting up a bar, bringing in ice, cutting lemons and limes, and doing other setup work I was ill prepared for. Other guests were clamoring for drinks, becoming impatient and believing me to be some sort of incompetent hired help. I kept hearing "Miss? Miss!" while I hustled to pour up beverages while dressed in a very expensive new dress that was rapidly becoming a stained expensive new dress. My rage was billowing, but I kept it in check, thinking that there must have been some sort of mix-up. I really couldn't believe that Tonya meant for me to be doing this and I didn't want to put a blot on her wedding so I continued my solo bartending act for the rest of the evening.

After several hours, I pushed one of the groomsmen behind the table so I could sit down for a minute, eat a little something, and hang out with some friends. Soon, though, I was back behind the table. I even ended up hauling boxes in and schlepping glasses to and from the kitchen, adding busboy to my job description. Any illusions that the bride didn't mean for me to be bartending ended when she hung out at the table for a minute chatting. At that point, I was done. Not caring what happened with Tonya, her wedding, or her bar, I sat down and enjoyed the final minutes of the reception and left all the booze out as self-serve. I even got funny looks from people, like, as the hired help I had no business just hanging out like that, and why wasn't I serving drinks?

This story exemplifies the fact that family and friends can be easily manipulated into service jobs. They willingly agree to all sorts of indignities for the sake of a wedding. They are under a powerful motivation not to bring attention to themselves by allegedly ruining poor Bridezilla's wedding day by declining the "honor" bestowed upon them. Knowing this, a bride can either use this to her selfish advantage or unselfishly take care in how she manages her volunteer labor force to avoid abusing them.

When I was younger, I fell victim to this ploy twice and have since witnessed others in similar straits. We get asked to do a specific job that, on the face of it, is not all that substantive in terms of time commitment. But upon arrival at the reception venue, we end up getting corralled into working our backsides off for hours on end, sometimes never seeing a minute of the reception from the confines of the kitchen. I've learned to say, "No, thank you," when asked to work for what amounts to an amateur caterer who doesn't know how to manage a surprised volunteer staff. Make sure you have someone who knows what he or she is doing to organize your reception and its catering and other support functions. Don't ever ask someone to do a small job and let it become a big job. You really shouldn't ask in the first place, so don't let someone who volunteered for a small job get rooked into doing a huge one for which he or she isn't prepared. These are your honored guests, not your servant lackeys!

In some cultures, it is an honor for a certain person to perform a particular service. For example, in the southeastern United States, pouring punch or serving cake is a highly sought-after honor reserved for close relatives. The local newspaper's account of the wedding ceremony and reception may in fact name these people as the honorary servers. If you do ask people to serve in a specific area, be very certain to state exactly what it is they are being asked to do, and don't let the task grow into something they will resent or regret agreeing to.

Rule 14: Transportation

Several years ago, my ex-boyfriend, Darling Dave, invited me to the wedding of his best friend, Bob Brainless. Bob and I had gone to a large high school together, so we were vague acquaintances. Bob was marrying Heather Hotter-Than-You, a rich only child who believed God should solicit her for advice on how to run the world.

Fast-forward to the day of the wedding. Darling Dave is the best man and I am the (last-minute) cake cutter. (A job I'm not fond of, but I, of course, accepted with a smile on my face. I wasn't asked out of friendship, obviously— she wanted to keep me occupied so she could introduce Dave to her out-of-town girlfriends.) After the ceremony, I discovered the bride and groom had hired a bus to take the guests to the reception. Since I had come with Dave (who drives a difficult stick shift), I'd be stranded if I didn't ride the bus (and there was plenty of room). Heather erupted when Dave asked her, so he informed her that he would drive both of us to the reception in his car. The groom wouldn't hear of it and insisted I ride with them. I was unaware of all the bickering. Dave just claimed me out in the foyer and led me to the bus. During the bus ride, Heather sat with her bridesmaids and whispered, glaring at me. I ignored her and talked to the guys. Finally, not being able to control herself any more and obviously irritated that I had not taken the "bait" and asked her what was wrong, she tottled over to me and said, "You know, I don't even want you on this bus with me—Bob made me take you. All the other bridesmaids had to leave their husbands behind and the groomsmen had to leave their wives behind—but oh, no! That just wouldn't work for you, would it!?"

Everyone looked embarrassed. I informed her that it was not possible for me to leave the bus now—regardless of how much I wanted to—but if she was sure that she couldn't bear another minute with me in the same vehicle, she had my blessing to fling herself off the back end after it had picked up speed. The groom came to calm her down. It was then that I finally noticed rings on the hands of most of the wedding party—they truly had had to leave spouses (and kids) behind and most of them were from out of town.

It gets worse.

I had thought the reception was a few miles away from the church, and I asked Dave where we were going. He informed me that Heather wanted to take the wedding party on a tour of the local college campus bars that she and Bob had hung out at during college. I was really surprised as I knew that everyone else had headed over to the reception thinking we were right behind them. The others in the wedding party were surprised too. One bridesmaid indicated that she had to return to the reception now—she was breastfeeding! The bride pulled her to the front of the bus and whispered to her animatedly and the nursing bridesmaid just looked glum. We had heard numerous times (from the bride) that this was "Her Day" and I can only assume that this was the "speech" the offender received too. The bride had arranged drinks and gifts for each of her attendants at each stop and had the photographer follow us to take photographs of the wedding party. The party bus parade added up to nearly two hours of barhopping—while friends and family cooled their heels at the reception. When we finally arrived at the dance hall, nearly half the guests had left. Most of the members of the wedding party had small kids, and several of their spouses (after finding out there had not been a wreck and after discovering what was going on) got disgusted and took their kids to the hotel to let them swim and get them to bed. The bride was livid—but who

could blame them? I cut the cake and then Dave and I left to take in a late
movie, thereby managing to salvage some fun out of an exhausting evening.

In a completely unrelated development, Dave and I were married last year.
While we were kneeling at the communion bench, he leaned over and said, "By
the way . . . I've rented this bus. . . ." His voice was picked up by his body mike
and broadcast to everyone in the church. I could hear my dad laughing from the
front row—our wedding party nearly lost it . . . (except for Bob).

Transportation is often one of those details to which the least attention is given but which can cause all sorts of problems. Tales
abound on www.etiquettehell.com of family members, bridesmaids,
parents, and spouses of the bridal party abandoned at the church with
no ride to the reception. A common error is that all the bridesmaids,
the bride, and her parents arrive at the church in a rented limo, which
then takes only the bride and groom to the reception. Bridesmaids and
Mom and Dad are left with no way to get to the reception unless by
prior arrangement to go with others.

If you rent a bus or limo that is solely for the bridal party, make
sure your attendants know this several days in advance so the spouse
or significant other can make the proper arrangements. The next logical consideration is that if you do arrange for transportation solely
for the bridal party, you shouldn't monopolize them for hours away
from their loved ones and family while you lead them on a wild ride
of bridal excess and self-absorption.

Rule 15: Treat the Vendors with Kindness

I remember one wedding in detail where the bride ran rampant throughout the
whole affair, scrutinizing every action of every staff member. When I arrived

to DJ, I found my DJ table a bit askew ... CDs were lined up for me to play. An angry note complained that there was no extra wireless microphone. When I met the bride, I knew then why my table was the way it was. She had gone over to the equipment, pulled out the music she wanted played, and ransacked the table for an extra mike (that she did not have in her contract, which I held in my hand). She stressfully told me how she wanted to be announced and how her bridal party was to be announced. After her grand gala entrance, she sat for dinner, and I had the displeasure of being located directly across from the head table, where she spent the evening shooting me evil looks.

The waitstaff had it no easier. One of them commented to me how she had requested a different server for her at the head table because she found the first's "odor" to be offensive. She then went into the kitchen to inquire why her dinner wasn't hot enough, and said she would revoke payment if her evening wasn't perfect. She yelled at the bartender for refusing to give her her own personal bottle of scotch to be shared at the head table. Then the music was not loud enough for the songs she liked, but was too loud for the songs she didn't. I didn't play the songs in the right order. I was playing too many slow songs. Then too many fast songs. Then not enough oldies. I personally think she would have preferred to have done the deejaying. She was over at my table more than I would have liked, but I knew the waitstaff were having their share too.

Your vendors are usually not the enemy. They come to work at each wedding knowing they are dealing with a bride and relations who may be highly emotional and even volatile. It is the vendor's job to make sure that everything goes according to the bride's wishes, as specified in the contract signed months previously. It is one's right to demand service if one has paid for said service. It is quite another to harass, belittle, and insult the "hired help" and treat them as if they are robots who were misprogrammed and are wreaking havoc on your day because the cookie display wasn't out at precisely nine P.M.; the waitress didn't hustle fast enough when you wanted a drink, or the DJ played a song that you absolutely *hate* but forgot to place on the do-not-play list. Your vendors are human beings and should be treated so. Every wedding at which they work, their boss, the bride, changes. It's your choice whether to be a benevolent boss who graciously says, "Thank you," and treats everyone with respect, or to be a tyrant who's busy telling others how to do their job, and proclaiming how *wrong* everything is, rather than enjoying yourself.

Rule 16: Place Cards: It's a Person, Not a Place

My fiancé's brother got married in September of 2001. At the time, my fiancé and I were not yet engaged, but had been seeing each other for three and a half years and living together for two of those years. I had attended just about every family function and socialized with his brother and his fiancée on a number of occasions. So, you can imagine that I was a little hurt when the wedding invitation arrived at our apartment addressed to "Mr. D and Guest." If the situation had been reversed, I would have addressed the invite to both of them. They knew my name and that there was absolutely no possibility D would be bringing anyone else. So, I was a little upset, but I got over it, and we RSVP'd that we would both be attending by writing both of our names on the RSVP card.

I arrive at the reception site and wait in line to get up to the place card table to find my name so I would know where to sit. When I finally make it up to the table, I discover that my name is nowhere to be found on any of the place cards. I scour them a couple of times to no avail. I then notice that there are a lot of place cards on the table that are simply labeled "And Guest," which I could only assume were supposed to be paired with the place cards with actual names on them immediately in front of them. My problem with this was that D was in the wedding party and therefore did not have a place card. How was I supposed to know which "And Guest" was supposed to be me?

There was still a line for the place card table behind me, so I stepped aside. At this point, I was fuming mad and had no idea what to do. So I went and sat in my car for a while to calm down and waited for basically everyone except for the bridal party to have taken their seats. I walked back in and surveyed the room and just sat down at the table with the greatest number of empty seats—the one with the highest table number, the "reject" table. I could only assume that this was where I was meant to be seated since they couldn't do me the dignity of actually putting my name on a place card.

The bridal party arrives at the reception and is introduced. During the break between the introductions and dinner, my fiancé comes over and finds me and says, "Why aren't you sitting with my parents like you should be?" Apparently, he had asked his brother and he had told him that I was meant to be sitting with their parents, but they had devised absolutely no way for me to know this. So, now I feel like I have insulted his parents because I was not sitting with them. It was horrible and I have never been so insulted, hurt, and angry all at the same time.

Place cards can be a blessing or a curse. The aforementioned story is just one example of why "And Guest" on an invitation can be fraught with so many possible ways to offend people or cause misunderstandings. Significant others who have been in relationships for an extended period of time, or the engaged partner, should *always* have a place card written in their name just as you would include them by name in the invitation.

One of the pitfalls to assigned seating is that some guests will creatively rearrange the place cards to suit their seating preferences. Once this happens, there is little you can graciously do to alter the situation so it's best to go with the flow. Other guests, particularly family, may object to their location, since proximity to the happy couple is equated with how close the guests' relationship is with the bride and groom. Too far from the bridal couple and it can be viewed as a deliberate slight. If you have arranged seating, make a valiant effort not to use it as a petty means to grade your guests based on relationship and consign the ones you really dislike to the outer limits of the room to dine with the bathroom attendant.

Rule 17: Restrain Thy Greed, Please

I am terribly ashamed of my conduct following the wedding / reception, though. Knowing virtually nothing about wedding etiquette, my husband and I started opening gifts as the reception was winding down.

This is becoming a more common occurrence, but it's not surprising. With the increased perception that weddings exist solely to add to the material assets of the marrying couple, people just can't seem to wait to dive right into the loot pile. What's worse, some couples will spend more time opening gifts at the reception than in actually conversing with their wedding guests. It screams, "Weddings are all about gifts to *me* so let's start opening all that booty right now!" If you must indulge your curiosity, arrange for a gift-opening brunch the next day with family.

Rule 18: Accidents Will Happen

As a wedding gift, my friend's aunt offered to make her wedding cake. She spent three days working on the three-tiered cake, completed with an additional cake on each side of the main one, from which "crystal" stairs went all the way to the top of the cake. The three-tiered cake was lifted by pillars and under it was placed a lighted fountain surrounded by fresh flowers complementing the bride's bouquet. It was beautiful and it was the bride's and her aunt's biggest pride.

After dinner the lights go down and the dancing starts. The thirteen-year-old junior bridesmaid, her younger brother, and the friend she brought to the wedding wander off. Her parents are too busy to keep an eye on them. Everyone is dancing and not paying attention to them. Everyone assumed, wrongfully, that at eleven and thirteen, they did not require to be babysat.

At some point in the evening, I'm mingling with some guests when the bride runs by us in tears, followed by the groom and her mother. It turns out that the bride had prepared small bottles of bubbles as a getaway toss and the junior bridesmaid poured one in the fountain of the wedding cake! The pressure of the fountain turned the soap into a mountain of foam, half the cake is sitting in it, and the photographer has not even taken the cake-cutting pictures yet! The only pictures of the cake my friend has in her album are the ones of her and her aunt proudly standing beside the cake before the reception.

Okay, so this wasn't an "accident." It was, however, typical of the dumb things that can go wrong with a wedding reception over which we have little control. Guests imbibing a bit too much and dancing like Vegas showgirls, cakes falling over, the tent leaking, the toss-away bouquet coming up missing. You have to keep a sense of humor about these situations rather than behaving as if a missing toss-away bouquet is the end of Western civilization. Some mishaps will make for great family stories years later and will certainly distinguish your wedding as different from the rest in a touchingly special way. As I mentioned earlier, you and your groom will set the mood for all the other participants, and if you are calm, even amused by the comedy of errors, your guests will follow your lead and take joy in the fact that all is well with the couple even if the reception has some unplanned glitches.

Brideweena's Checklist

1. Have I arranged transportation for the wedding party and parents to and from the ceremony and reception?

2. Have I arranged for some nibbles for guests while we are off taking photographs?

3. Do I have sufficient refreshments during the reception?

4. Does my reception venue have heat, air-conditioning, clean bathrooms, plenty of seating, and enough space for all my guests?

5. Have I planned for appropriate quantities of food for my guests?

6. Have I done a final check with the vendors without hassling them every other day?

7. Have I arranged for vegetarian meals for my non-meat-eating guests?

8. I didn't schedule our wedding during the ACC semifinals, did I?

9. Have I figured out the logistics of the receiving line, if I am having one?

10. Does the DJ have our "do not play" list and names of the bridal party?

11. Have I written a thank-you to exceptionally professional vendors who made the day flow so well?

Thank You Very Much

Gratitude is a fruit of great cultivation; you do not find it among gross people. —SAMUEL JOHNSON

THE PLANNING IS DONE, the wedding is over, and the honeymoon is fading into the warmly glowing horizon of memory. Now before you looms the biggest obstacle ever to face mortal man. Rising up to obscure the road ahead into marital bliss is the mountain of thank-you notes demanding your attention.

Of course, you should have been writing and mailing thank-you notes as you've been receiving the gifts so as not to be faced with this daunting task just when you'd really rather be canoodling with the new spouse.

Lesser humans have blanched at the thought of terminal hand fatigue and devised all manner of clever ways to avoid the inevitable stationery Everest—ignoring it, driving around it, anything other than just tackling it head-on.

But write them you must, lest you be burdened with a guilty chain that hangs on to your once good name like Jacob Marley's sins.

Rule 1: At Least Write the Little Buggers

The shower went off without a hitch, although the other bridesmaids didn't help at all except to "help" open the many gifts they received, and to pass out envelopes so the guests could self-address their own thank-you notes. The envelopes were used for a "raffle" for prizes. How tacky! I spent over $200 on a dress and shoes, not to mention the $100 gift I bought for them, and the $200 I chipped in for the shower. You'd think that she would at least take the time to address the envelopes herself and send out notes to everyone thanking them for the very nice gifts they received. But although most of the envelopes were already addressed, my sister did not send out thank-you notes to anyone.

In a previous chapter I've hashed out how tacky and lazy it is to get the wedding guests to address their own thank-you-note envelopes so I won't belabor the point again. However, to then not to bother sending them at all is *mucho* unbelievably ungrateful and, well, gross.

Rule 2: It's Not an Invoice

My husband and I were invited to a wedding in New York City with a reception to follow on a boat that would take us around the island. We attended the wedding. There were about forty guests. The boat ride was nice, there was dinner and dancing. It was fun.

We did not present a gift before or during the wedding. We had spent a sum of money getting to New York from Texas, and planned on waiting a few weeks to send something to the new couple. I knew, from my mother the etiquette queen, and from helping with my two sisters' huge weddings, that it is appropriate to give a gift up to one year after the wedding.

About two weeks after the wedding, a postcard arrived from the groom stating that unfortunately someone stole some of their gifts from the boat, and if we had given them a check, we should stop payment and send another one.

A couple of e-mails soon followed: "Hey, gee, did you hear we got ripped off?" We still didn't have the money to give our gift yet (about six weeks later now).

Another couple of weeks went by. A letter arrived from the groom with stronger words: "We spent $127 per person for the boat trip and dinner, and didn't expect to receive no gift."

By now my husband and I suspected the story about the theft was made up, and was a nudge to the non-gift-givers to pay up. We felt this was pretty rude, and wondered about the friendship. We also speculated that the newlyweds were having financial troubles, and instead of fighting with each other, they were blaming their wedding guests.

Finally, a handwritten letter arrived from the bride, whom we had met only that day. I can accurately quote: "That will be $250, please," following an admonition about how expensive the wedding was and how tacky it is to go to a wedding and not give a gift.

We have not heard from either of them since then. That was five years ago. I looked it up in several etiquette books: one year is appropriate. Unfortunately their "demand letter" gave us only two months.

This isn't just a faux pas; it's a murder scene where the relationship has been brutally massacred by the newlyweds for the mere pittance of $250.

After I started Etiquette Hell almost a decade ago, I never received such a story in all the thousands that people submitted. But all that changed in the last three years. Now I routinely get letters from people who tell of receiving what they think is a thank-you note, but opening it to find that the bride has sent them what is, in effect, an invoice for the total amount of the per-person cost of the reception. Reasons given for these invoices range anywhere from "Your gift was not enough to offset the cost of your meal" to "You RSVP'd and didn't attend and cost me XXX amount of money needlessly." Such audacious rudeness takes the breath away!

If you did your wedding planning with the philosophy that guests *owe* you a gift commensurate with the costs you are expending on the wedding, you've deceived yourself for many months. Just how are guests supposed to divine this monetary figure? By laying hands on the invitation and using their psychic powers to pick up the reception-cost vibes emanating from the ink? Even if you did have that delusion, giving voice to it by chastising guests who fail to meet your expectations is beyond tacky. It's conspicuously gross. You might as well slap an I'M A RUDE, GREEDY IDIOT sign on your forehead for the rest of your life.

Second, don't presume to know why a guest would RSVP in the affirmative and then not attend. You will invariably presume incorrectly. I've received stories from people who wanted to attend the wedding and had replied in the affirmative to the invitation, but something suddenly came up such as an illness or being called into work on an emergency that prevented them from going. Despite sending a nice wedding gift, within weeks they had received not a thank-you note but angry invoices demanding payment for the reception meal that went uneaten.

I know very well how frustrating it is to cater a nice reception, only to scan the banquet room noting the empty seats where place cards give away the names of the missing in action. However, under no circumstances can you vent your frustration via a mailed invoice. If you

are that concerned, call them and ask, "I was looking forward to seeing you at the wedding but I missed seeing you. Is everything okay?"
If it turns out they are the kind of friends who bail out of an invitation
in favor of something better having come along, politely acknowledge
any gift they gave you without reference to their missing-persons status and then resolve to strike them from your future guest lists. Some
people do deserve to be condemned to the social Etiquette Hell of
wondering why they never get invited anywhere or have so few friends.
You, however, do not need to sink down there with them by giving a
nasty response.

Using your thank-you notes for anything other than a gushingly
grateful acknowledgment of gifts or labor is crass, rude, obnoxious,
and ungrateful.

Rule 3: Right *Now*, This Very Minute

A few years ago, my mother received an invitation to a colleague's daughter's
(also a former student's) wedding. Because of her teaching schedule, she and my
father were unable to attend, but they made sure to inquire about the bride's
registry so that they might send a thoughtful gift. The bride's mother actually
asked my mom to purchase a specific item: a large, gaudy, expensive ceramic
cookie jar in the shape of a chicken (?!). My parents dutifully went to the store
to purchase the monstrosity even though it cost twice what they wanted (and
could reasonably be expected) to spend. They realized that there were several
variations on the model, and took great care to select one that the bride would
really like. The wedding came and went with no acknowledgment of the gift.
About ten months later, my mother asked the bride's mother whether the couple
had received the gift—mainly because they wanted to make sure they bought the
right chicken!! The bride's mother—an uptight, old-money Junior Leaguer who

always criticizes other women's manners—got very prickly and said that she wasn't sure.

Three weeks later, a very cursory thank-you note arrived. The mother actually had the gall to grudgingly say, "Well, she got it in under the deadline of a year!" when my mom acknowledged the note to her! First of all, isn't it the rule that guests have a year after a wedding to send a gift? Brides—or any recipient of a gift—should thank people ASAP! Who waits a year to acknowledge a kindness? The worst part is, my own wedding is coming up shortly. The colleague thoughtfully dropped off a gift at my house, but on her way out the door said, "Don't worry about a thank-you—save your energy for people who care about those things!" while shooting a very dirty look at my mom. Ouch!

The above story also illustrates an important time distinction between guests giving gifts and the recipient acknowledging them. It is correct that guests have upward of a year after the nuptials to bless the happy couple with a gift. It does not follow that you get a year to send out thank-you notes. It's probably the most commonly believed etiquette myth that I hear, but it is just that—a myth.

If you don't send out your thank-you notes promptly, say, within a month after the wedding at most, some guests will wonder whether you received the gifts and begin to worry. Other guests will marvel at the amazing alacrity with which you can endorse a check and get it deposited, compared to your lugubriousness in lifting pen to paper to thank them for their gift of money. If you have the time to rip open a wrapped gift, put it to use in the house and throw away the box and wrapping paper, you have enough time to write a thank-you note.

Immutable Fact of Life

Gimmy and Greedella had a beautiful baby girl but they were very upset that their church would not give them a baby shower! Finally, out of exasperation and tired of being polite, my mother told them, "Do you honestly think that the church members would give you a baby shower when you never sent out thank-you notes from the wedding shower?"

There is a wonderful quote by author Stephen R. Covey that goes, "While we are free to choose our actions, we are not free to choose the consequences of our actions." You can choose not to write any thank-you notes to those who gave wedding presents, but you don't get to choose the consequences your friends and family will inflict upon you. It is an immutable fact of life that ingratitude squelches the fountain of generosity. No one likes feeding an insatiably greedy and ungrateful humanoid.

Rule 4: Put Some Effort into It

My fiancé and I became good friends with a couple we met while in our marriage preparation classes for the Catholic church. Their wedding was a lavish hotel affair where they easily spent over $30K on the reception alone. We decided to buy them a nice expensive gift even though we were currently saving for our own wedding, which was three months later. Instead of getting a nice thank-you note for our gift, we received a letter printed off the computer that aside from having our names on the note, was not personalized at all. They didn't even bother to sign the letter either. I would think a hundred-dollar gift should at least get a signature.

Sometimes I wish I knew ahead of time just how lackadaisical a gift recipient is going to be, so I could tailor my gift giving accordingly. Just imagine if everyone put the same amount of effort into selecting a gift as some people do in expressing gratitude. The art of writing thank-you notes would be changed forever!

In my opinion, computer-generated and mass-mailed thank-you notes are not acceptable. To call it a "thank-you note" would be like calling a piece of dime-store jewelry a fine gemstone. It gets the sender off the hook by only the barest of legalistic definitions but leaves a rancid taste in the mouths of the recipients, who may wonder if they have been shanghaied into funding a gift orgy that gets acknowledged by what is essentially a receipt.

A considerate, appropriately grateful thank-you note includes the givers' name, some comments about the intended usage of the gift, and a handwritten signature. The following is *not* an example of a good thank-you note:

> *Thank you for sharing in our special day. Thank you for your gift of money.*
> *Love, Bridastein and Groomly*

As the recipient of this terse thank-you note observed, "This just screams class!" Gratitude and the ability to express it cogently is a cultivated talent that everyone should master proficiently. The following is a real thank-you note I received and demonstrates all aspects of a well-written note. Handwritten, personal address, talks about the gift, personally signed.

Dear Jeanne and Leigh,

Thank you so much for the homemade kitchen items. The apron and hot mitts are wonderful since they are even my kitchen colors!! I can't wait to use them. Thanks also for the hand-crocheted dishcloths and soap. They are so pretty I'm scared to use them but I will. Thanks also for the Pyrex dish. I've not seen one with the basket weave on it before. Your gift was also one of the rare ones that Patrick actually noticed. He was excited about every piece from apron to dish.

Thank you!!

Jennifer

A good thank-you note, as Dale Carnegie has pointed out, includes three key elements: appreciation of the giver, appreciation of the gift, and appreciation of the uses to which you plan to put the gift. If you hit those three, you'll engender warm fuzzies in the giver that will last for months. Tell them how thoughtful and helpful and special they are. Tell them how cool the gift itself is and how you plan to use it and gain benefit from it, thus from their kindness and consideration. You'll help them be glad they gave the gift and build an even greater bond with them at the same time, leaving everyone richer.

Of course, no matter how well you write and send out your thank-you notes, there is always some kooky guest who takes issue with it:

I work for a very small company and have to share my office with my supervisor. As we got along pretty well, I was sure to invite him when I got married.

Although he and his wife could not come, they were kind enough to send a wedding gift. They gave us a lovely set of wineglasses. We were so surprised and thrilled. After the wedding, I took great care to write everyone a personalized thank-you note. A few days after I mailed them off, he told me that they had received our note. I said I was glad, smiled, and went on working on a project. Then he said, "You know, we thought it was overdone. . . . I mean, my wife and I could almost imagine you actually using the glasses, you know, touching them lovingly. . . . Well, it was quite crass, actually. You could have simply said thank you."

I was stunned. I have never heard of critiquing a thank-you note that someone put some thought into. Please put my supervisor in Etiquette Hell where he belongs.

With pleasure I hereby cast your idiotic supervisor into Etiquette Hell. One woman wrote to me of diligently writing out her thank-you notes in record time only to get severely chastised by a coworker who claimed such speediness reflected an unnatural obsession with gift grubbing by the bride. Perhaps these people are so deprived of ever having seen a finely crafted thank-you note that when the real McCoy arrives, it is viewed with deep suspicion. Gee, aren't all thank-you notes supposed to be terse, impersonal, and insincere? Where these people get these odd and mythic interpretations of etiquette is a mystery, but they are nonetheless deceived in their opinions and should be ignored. The remaining 99.9 percent of your guests will be practically dancing a jig of joy that the state of the world is not as bad as we all thought, as long as one person has a grateful heart.

Rule 5: No Bait and Switch

The bride and groom decided to hand-deliver to each person attending the reception, before the food was served at the reception, along with the Jordan almonds in netting, a preprinted thank-you, stating, "Thank you for attending our wedding and the thoughtful gift."

Don't think for even a minute that favors with generic thanks attached will get you off the hook of executing a proper expression of appreciation for gifts received. It falls under the "mass-produced gift receipt" mentioned earlier and completely lacks any personalization. That also includes preprinted scrolls guests are supposed to pick up at the reception, or cutesy little place-card frames with a preprinted thank-you inside.

The Wedding Consultation

Brideweena: Oh, beloved husband of mine? Here's your pile of thank-you notes that need to be written!

Curtis: What? I thought this was *your* job! After all, most everything people gave us were girly gifts. You know, oven mitts, blender, can opener, crocheted toilet paper roll covers. Foofy, girly-girl things like that.

Brideweena: Oh, no you don't, bucko! If you think you are going to weasel out of this and leave it all for me to do by myself, you have another think coming. You are just as much a beneficiary of our guests' generosity as I am and we will share the obligation to thank our guests profusely.

Curtis: Can't I just be the official envelope and stamp licker?

Brideweena: Nope. Here's your list of people and addresses to write to. If we work together, we can finish in a night or two. Just the two of us huddled head to head at the table, comparing notes, as we share this opportunity to express our appreciation to family and friends for the love they showed us with their gifts.

Curtis: That sounds so . . . romantic!

Rule 6: Silent Gratitude Isn't Much Use to Anyone

Reasons given to me by an otherwise darling and sweet friend for her decision not to write thank-you cards—it's too expensive to buy cards to send out; there are too many people for her to bother (ninety to a hundred); she doesn't expect or ask for any presents, so she shouldn't have to thank anyone; the cake boxes have "Thank You" printed on them, that should be enough; she is showing some of her overseas relatives around the city, that's enough of a thank-you for them; her wedding isn't going to be very formal, she thinks thank-yous are only for formal weddings.

Uh-oh, I feel it coming on. It's welling up in my gut like a volcano of peptic acid. It's another severe outbreak of Ornery Guest Syndrome! I suppose as wedding guests we could take the following perspective as well:

- It's too expensive to buy wedding gifts.
- There are too many weddings this year for me to bother giving everyone a wedding gift.
- My empty card says "Congratulations on your marriage!" That should be enough.
- I babysat the bride when she was a snot-nosed bratling and wiped countless poopy butts while diapering her, that's enough of a gift for her.

It isn't "darling and sweet" to have such a cavalier attitude about other people's generosity and your responsibility to acknowledge it. One excuse I've heard so many times is that, "They are family, they know I appreciate their gift," with the definition of "family" extended to include close friends, church members, and even coworkers. Unless these people are endowed with psychic abilities or are ultrasensitive to the silent gratitude vibes emanating from your person, no, they don't know. To presume to know that everyone of your acquaintance wouldn't mind your dereliction of note-writing duty is the height of arrogance and hubris.

But that is hardly the worst case of presumptions about thank-you notes. Read on.

My friend Mary got married a few years ago and asked me to be a bridesmaid. I was very excited and got involved with the normal bridesmaid-type activities: shopping for dresses, planning her shower. I didn't get a thank-you for my shower gift (or for helping to throw the shower), but I figured she was busy with wedding plans. I got her a very nice gift from her registry for her wedding. Months went by and no thank-you note. When I saw my friend again almost six months after the wedding, I asked her if she had received my wedding gift. (I had the store ship it directly to her house.) She replied that she had received it and had decided that part of the wedding party's gift to her was that she didn't have to write thank-you notes to us!

First presuming she was owed more gifts from her wedding party and then presuming she can decide what that gift is and finally "taking" that gift; does the audacity of this bride just take your breath away? I confess to sucking it in like a vacuum cleaner at first reading. I'm allergic to brides like this. I break out in a severe case of Over My Dead Body Syndrome, which handicaps me from ever bestowing the fruits of my labors on their ungrateful carcasses again. It is a kindness, in a way, not to burden these people with gifts that would require them to write a note of gratitude.

Rule 7: Labor Is Not Free

My wife and I got married after I graduated from college in April of 2000. A friend of my wife's mother graciously agreed to make the wedding dress as a present. All she asked in return was that we provide the material (less than $40) and give her a wedding picture of the dress. You see, the friend was a professional seamstress and wished to add a picture of the dress she would make to her portfolio.

Did I mention that my wife was living on the opposite coast from her family and this seamstress at the time?

Several months before the wedding, my wife made it out for a visit to her family for a week. During that week, all the fittings were made and the basic part of the dress created. When the wedding rolled around, my wife had a beautiful, hand-crafted, professional dress. We couldn't have been more grateful to this friend for her service.

Eight months later, my wife and I were finally back in California to visit her parents and we made a trip to visit this seamstress who had made such a special gift for us. We handed her a beautifully framed picture of us as a couple as well as an eight-by-ten professional picture of my wife in the dress for the seamstress's portfolio.

This wonderful lady almost started crying. She told us that she has made a total of ten dresses for people as gifts, each time asking for only a picture in return. She said that we were the first couple to ever give her the desired picture.

My wife and I were floored. A picture seemed like such a small token to repay such a lavish present.

The next day at a church meeting, this seamstress found my wife to thank her again. She said it somewhat reminded her of the story in the Bible of Jesus healing the ten lepers and only one returning to thank Him.

If you have been so fortunate as to have been spared some wedding expense because someone has given a gift of his or her time, you have a double responsibility to express your gratitude. Gifts of labor very often can value in the hundreds, if not thousands, of dollars but they are overlooked because either there is not a tangible, wrapped gift or people simply have no concept of the labor involved to place a high value on it. The above scenario is not uncommon to me at all. I used to cater wedding receptions at cost for friends as a gift, asking only for a few photos from the photographer of how the buffet table looked.

Despite saving them thousands of dollars for a comparable wedding reception, I have yet to have anyone give me their photographer's photo as requested. I don't even bother asking anymore and just bring my own camera. I've given the brides a list of people who cheerfully volunteered to help serve at their receptions, and some write every single person a grateful note while others couldn't be bothered. It's the latter variety that leads me into temptation to stray right into Etiquette Hell. We don't have to give them this gift of our time and effort but, having done so, one would think the resulting response would be a bit more effusive.

Here is a fine example of a thank-you note expressing appreciation for the gifts of labor that made the wedding special:

Dear Jeanne, Leigh, Zack, and Lucia,

Thank you so much for the tireless hours you spent preparing for and putting together a wedding reception that surpassed any expectations we could have had.

Jeanne, your experience and the time you put into thinking up just the right way for traffic to flow was such a blessing. It all turned out so beautifully and we know that was because of your commitment to do it all to the best of your ability. Your efforts not only blessed us, but they blessed our guests as well.

Leigh, Zack, and Lucia, what a blessing your willing labor was! Each of you were so eager and expressed such delight in helping us and your mother. You are an example to those around you of excellence in service, and many of us "adults" could learn from your cheerfulness.

Finally, Tim, thank you for sparing us your family as they sought to serve. What an encouragement and example they have been!

With love, Joy and Michael

Now you don't know Michael and Joy at all, but doesn't reading that note cause your innards to just gush with ooey-gooey affection and fond regard for them? It has that effect on me. While you may not intend to elicit dramatic intrinsic reactions in your guests, consider that such thank-you notes can have the effect of strengthening relationships to the mutual edification of all parties. You can't ever go wrong with a well-crafted thank-you note.

Brideweena's Checklist

1. Have I written thank-you notes to everyone who gave us a wedding gift?

2. Have I written thank-you notes to everyone who gave us a gift of labor?

3. Do my thank-you notes include a personalized message that acknowledges the gift, the giver, and uses of the gift?

4. Did I hand-address the envelopes myself?

NINE

In the Family's Way

God gives us our relatives—thank God we can choose
our friends. —Michel Eyquem de Montaigne

THE OLD AXIOM IS TRUE. You can choose your friends but
family is forever. It's also true that familiarity breeds con-
tempt where the family ties become an excuse for presumptions, assumptions, and plain old garden-variety taking things for
granted.

A wedding can bring out the best or the worst in people, but either
way, nearly every mother of the bride has definite ideas about her
daughter's wedding. Your mother may want to experience the wedding
she never had while your father is so out of the loop to be worthless.
Meanwhile your future in-laws have different expectations of what
they consider the perfect wedding. You are required to be the most ac-
complished diplomat, under circumstances that would try a Henry
Kissinger, in order to prevent Family World War III. It's enough to
drive a sane person to madness.

The art of compromising to keep the family peace requires you
pick your battles carefully. Now is not the time to be a control freak

over trivial matters that no one will remember in three years. Stand firm on the parts that matter the most and cave graciously to family wishes on those that aren't worth dying for.

Of course, the civil bride executes her decisions with decorum, grace, and nerves of steel. Screaming, manipulations, and snotty comebacks all diminish the dignity of the person from whose mouth those vile communications flow.

Rule 1: Honor Where Honor Is Due

Ten minutes before wedding: Best man (brother of groom) comes up to my mom and asks for a corsage for his aunt. My mom had bought corsages for all the aunts and grandmothers on both sides. No one had mentioned this aunt. The wedding was about to start and there were more important things to attend to, and the best man insisted again about the corsage. My mom came a bit unglued. Turns out she was his uncle's new girlfriend and about twenty years younger than the uncle. She did not get a corsage.

There is a temptation to give every family member and special friend a corsage or boutonniere. People are always trying to pin a corsage on me, the wedding coordinator. Invariably someone gets left out or forgotten and the oversight is viewed as evidence of an evil conspiracy. Corsages and boutonnieres really belong to immediate family and grandparents to distinguish them as worthy of honor. By giving every Tom, Dick, and second cousin three times removed some flower token, it degrades the honor reserved for parents and grandparents. You aren't going to Etiquette Hell if you give everyone in the family a flower, but you will dramatically increase your odds of offending someone. Do you want to take that risk?

Rule 2: Evil Etiquette

Later in the evening I see my fiancé's grandmother pull him aside and talk to him quite rapidly for a few minutes, and then I see him shake his head and pull away while she has a hand on his coat sleeve. He did manage to get away without too much fuss. I asked him later if everything was all right and he told me that she had pulled him aside to tell him that to address invitations with "and Guest" was the traditional, more formal and polite way to address invitations to unmarried couples, and that also they wanted to give him the option of bringing someone other than me if he wanted to. Who else would he have brought? If he wasn't taking his fiancée, was he supposed to find a date?

Be aware that family members can attempt to manipulate the plans by claiming "proper etiquette." They hold the threat of social ostracism over the victim's head, claiming superior knowledge of etiquette. Mothers, grandmothers, and even aunts are notorious for contorting etiquette rules to suit a personal preference or to bolster their position in favor of some "tradition" you find disagreeable. It's times like this when you need to do what is right, not what you are told to do.

Rule 3: Some People Are Just Wrong

Last week I sent out my save-the-date e-mails. To my surprise, I received this e-mail last night in response from a cousin of my fiancé:

We don't want to come to your wedding. We feel that you two were very insensitive with the date that you chose. February is too close after Christmas, so no one is going to buy you any gifts, not to mention that any normal person is not going to drive in the snow! Why couldn't you have your wedding in the summer like everyone else? We enjoy summer weddings, and just can't understand why you decided to have a winter wedding.

If you decide to change it to June, July, or August, please let us know and we will be happy to make the *long* drive.

Makes you wonder if she was a former Bridezilla, now morphed into a Cousinzilla. It's all about me and what makes me comfortable! You are under no obligation to compromise for people like this. Either ignore the comments or send them a nice note saying, "Dear Cousin, We're sorry you both won't be attending our wedding. Have a lovely summer! Love, Brideweena." It probably would be more polite to add, "We'll both miss seeing you at the wedding," but if you have to tell a lie to write that, it's best to leave it off than be found guilty of insincerity.

Rule 4: The Grandstanding Mother

During one particular wedding shopping excursion, I was required to buy the bride lunch, during which festive occasion I was treated to dramatics about how her future mother-in-law hated her and would try to ruin her wedding. The bride even managed to work in some self-pitying tears of maltreatment over her lunch of popcorn shrimp and French fries. I'd met her future mother-in-law, whom I found self-involved and pushy, and I was beginning to wonder if the son hadn't managed to find a gal just like dear old Mom. Dawned the day of the wedding, which was to be held in July in a small church with no air-conditioning. It was easily in the high nineties by noon. The wedding was to be at 1:30. Not 1:00, not 2:00, but 1:30, because everyone *knows you can only get married when the minute hand is on the upsweep. A hundred sweating people were packed into the hot pews, using bulletins to fan themselves. The 1:30 mark passed, and everyone waited, shifting in their seats, straining in the stillness for a breeze from one of the small windows.*

One forty-five comes and goes. One fifty-five. Two o'clock.

Just then, the mother-in-law, who sincerely doesn't like or approve of the bride, pulled in with a lame excuse about getting lost. (Their hotel was ten minutes away.) A supreme grandstand maneuver and the bride had been aced. And knew it. Many tears were shed in the bridal-preparation chamber, during which time all of the guests were required to wait until 2:30, when the all-important minute hand was on the upsweep again.

Stories abound of mothers pulling this stunt. Shame on them! You can expect similar passive-aggressive obstacles to your happiness throughout your marriage too. The solution to this is not to give someone the power to do this. You are strong, civil, and gracious! The wedding starts on time, regardless of who is there or not. Wait ten minutes if you have to to give them the benefit of the doubt, but no longer than fifteen minutes. And then the show goes on because more people will be inconvenienced by a late wedding than one person will in being late.

I also wouldn't give anyone the satisfaction of knowing they had caused me emotional distress with their ploy. Dramatic displays of emotion reward the smug evil mother-in-law from Etiquette Hell, and we really don't want to give her that pleasure, do we? So much better to greet her with pleasantries and thwart any gleeful gloating she thought she was going to enjoy secretly at your expense. Don't misconstrue your civility as an endorsement of someone's bad behavior. No, this is war and you don't surrender to the enemy any advantage over you. If they want to wallow in the gutter of pettiness, go ahead and let them. It doesn't mean you have to lose your dignity and take a flying leap into the mud hole with them. Be civil and inwardly triumphant that you have chosen to rise above it while the evil relative has established her residency in Etiquette Hell. Mental pictures of diabolical in-laws rotisserating over the Etiquette Hell grill with the flames of shame licking at them should elicit sufficient satisfaction to thwart even the most evil of desires to say nasty things.

Rule 5: Don't Make Them Do It

I went to the wedding of a family friend many years ago that will forever be etched in my memory. The groom was a friend of my father's, Martin, who was marrying a divorcée with two daughters. The previous marriage had lasted ten years but the divorce had been final for at least two when the couple met. Two years later, they decided to get married. The bride, Valerie, had two daughters, aged fifteen and seventeen. They were not happy about the marriage as they had always harbored dreams of their parents reuniting (though why, at those ages, they were still living in a dream world, I do not know, as their parents could barely stand to be in the same room together!).

So, it's the wedding day and Valerie's daughters are the bridesmaids. They walk down the aisle in their big, boofy dresses (with serious butt bows but, hey, it was the late eighties), completely stone-faced. Not great, but the best was to come. As the groom and bride begin to exchange their vows, the girls start to weep. Not little weeping either, with just tears—no, whopping great moaning and wailing weeping. You could barely hear the minister over their hysterics.

*As young teenagers, my brothers and I thought it hilarious as everyone in the church began to shift awkwardly. (We were trained better, though, and didn't laugh out loud, especially with Mum right next to us!) But wow—there's a lesson. If they don't want to be in the wedding—*don't *make them bridesmaids. Years on, I look back and think what brats they were—at fifteen and seventeen, they knew they were embarrassing their mum and just didn't care. Sadly, the marriage ended within three years and Martin married a lovely lady without children.*

These are older children, but the same applies for all minor-aged children: don't presume they support this marriage and want to demonstrate that support by standing up for you. Requiring that children participate in a wedding for the sake of appearances or for some symbolic family unity rite is a pathetic misuse of your parental authority. Of course, if they want to participate in the wedding, by all means include them, as appropriate.

Rule 6: The Parents Giveth, and the Parents Taketh Away

When we first announced that we were getting married, my mother-in-law said that she would pay for the liquor at our wedding. Over the next year and a half until the wedding finally happened, she would repeatedly get offended at some imagined slight by us or my family, and announce that she wasn't going to come to the wedding and she wasn't going to pay for the liquor. The last time she did this was only about three days before the wedding. My husband was in a big panic. I said, "I don't care. I don't need to have booze at my wedding. If anybody asks me why we don't have any, I will tell them exactly why." In the end, she had only about half the amount of money that we needed and we had to ask my dad for more money for liquor, after he was already paying for most of the reception.

This is a common scenario, with some parents playing games with their gifts of money. It can be even worse between divorced parents. The first thing you should remember is that your parents do not owe you a lovely wedding or cash for you to have the wedding of your dreams. If you were presuming they did, you can gain bridal equilibrium by readjusting your expectations right now. Fulfilling their parental obligations to children does not extend to funding a wedding extravaganza. To avoid these conflicts, pay for the entire wedding yourselves even though that may mean scaling back the plans to reflect the reality of a limited budget. Otherwise, you may have too much emotional investment in that cash bar and it gets used as manipulative leverage either against the other parent or you. You can defuse the potential manipulative value by calling the bluff, as the bride above wanted to do, and just do without. Your guests are not going to shrivel up into little dust balls from alcohol deprivation, nor are you going to have a ruined wedding day or marriage if the flowers are not abundant and expensive.

Rule 7: There Is No Pleasing Some People

On discussing the seating plan of our impending wedding with my then future mother-in-law, she refused to be seated with my parents at the parents' table. Her reason? Her actual words: "When you sit next to someone you don't know, you end up having a boring time." I suppose the idea of the wedding being an opportunity to get to know her newly related counterparts, or perhaps organizing a rehearsal dinner to spend time with them beforehand, didn't cross her mind.

Disappointed at her attitude and various other snubs she had given my parents, I juggled the difficult seating plan to accommodate their wishes. On the

*big day they had the gall to complain bitterly that they hadn't been seated at the
parents' table. You just can't please some people.*

Some people will create all kinds of problems, and no matter how
you contort yourself to accommodate them, it still isn't enough. They
are the Perpetually Offended and they inflict their tyranny wantonly.
Your best defense is constant communication and documentation.
"Mom, I think I understand what you are saying and here is what I
planned according to your wishes. I'm putting you and Dad at a table
with your relatives. Is that satisfactory?" Record the date of the conversation and the comments. If you fear future divergence of recollec-
tions, then either confirm the conversation in an e-mail or have the
conversation in the presence of a third person who can verify what is
agreed upon. At some point, you may have to lay down the law and
declare that the arrangements are what they are based on what people
have communicated to you and you are not changing them. It goes
without saying that this gets communicated sans any demon-bride attitudes. It is possible to be quite firm yet terribly sweet in your de-
meanor. "I'm so sorry, Mrs. Mom, but I made the decisions based on
everyone's input and simply cannot change them at this date."

Yes, someone will be PO'd at you no matter how fair and just you
were in the decisions you made, but there isn't any reason why you
have to surrender your soul to the tyranny of the Perpetually Offended.

Rule 8: The Invasion of the Etiquette Snatchers

*When my husband and I were married, we chose not to register, since it felt
uncomfortably like writing letters to Santa when we were kids. We also chose to*

forgo "traditions" like fishing out the garter with teeth, tossing the garter and bouquet, and auctioning kisses from the bride. We did not have a formal dance or a disc jockey, because we have both been to many weddings where the dance floor stayed empty and the music overpowered conversation. Instead, we hired a string quartet from the local university to play during dinner and the reception. We cleared a space in front of the quartet so that those who wanted to dance could do so.

My father-in-law was angry at our choices, and warned us that people who gave up an evening to come to a wedding expected to be entertained. We assured him that we appreciated his input, but thought that it would all come together nicely. I thought that was the end of the matter.

The reception went well until after dinner. After we finished cutting the cake, a contingent of my in-laws came to the table to give me a good dressing-down. My husband's grandfather told me that because we had been "too cheap" to have a proper dance, he had no choice but to take his gift back. I told him that we appreciated his coming nonetheless, and he stomped out.

My husband's aunt said that by choosing not to have a dollar dance or an auction, I was essentially saying that I was too good to accept the generosity of his family. I admitted that I hadn't realized how much the giving meant to her family—but I was uncomfortable with the traditions, as I had not grown up with them.

A second aunt asked me why we even bothered to have a wedding if we weren't going to throw the bouquet or the garter. She said that she expected us to behave like a bride and a groom, instead of dinner party hosts. My mother-in-law whipped out the same line. "If you didn't take the wedding preparations seriously, how can we believe that you take marriage to our son seriously?" I thought I was going to cry.

My husband and I decided to appease our guests by dancing in the space we had cleared near the musicians. The wedding party joined in too. Some guests drifted in and out as the reception went on. Most of the guests seemed to be having a good time, and told us so when they left. In retrospect, my husband's family probably interpreted our toned-down wedding plans as an implicit rejection of them and their preferences. I'm not sure how I could have reconciled everybody's wishes.

An increasingly common occurrence in wedding planning is that two people from two very different cultures marry. What one family may view as completely acceptable and even required for a respectable wedding, the other family would view with horror and discomfort. Sometimes, there is no way to reconcile your wedding plans with the outrageous expectations of one side of the family. The above groom's side of the family seems to have forgotten that traditionally it is the bride and her family that plans and hosts the wedding and reception. As a group, they are guilt-manipulative and self-centered, thinking only of what their side of the family deems to be a respectable wedding without even remotely considering what the other half of the guests may enjoy. And if you think it will stop at the wedding, buckle your seat belt, because the ride has just begun. These same people will demand you spend every Thanksgiving and Christmas with their side of the family with no thought whatsoever that there exists an entire other family who has a vested interest in celebrating with the Happy Couple too. The wedding is just the start of a tug-of-war that can continue for decades.

Accommodating everyone's "wishes" doesn't mean you should sell your soul into Etiquette Hell by compromising on your principles. If people need a dollar dance or some tacky auction of kisses to ignite their generosity, there is a serious screw loose in their motivations. These sick people want you to perform like a trained seal to get their miserable money and you are better off without it. Etiquette doesn't require us to make boorish people feel comfortable. In some situations, making them uncomfortable can be the best solution to a dilemma.

Rule 9: When Mom Is an Etiquette Nazi

My then fiancé and I had a whirlwind romance. Four months after meeting each other, we were engaged, and planning a justice-of-the-peace wedding three months later. I am not religious, and he doesn't have a lot of friends and family. We wanted to keep it simple and planned on a barbecue, not a reception, the following spring. My mom saw this as a faux pas and told me that it was inconsiderate to expect family and friends to wait six months to celebrate our marriage. I sort of agreed, but also told her that we couldn't afford to save up for a reception in three months. I know everyone is wondering why we couldn't just wait until the following spring to get married. I guess we can blame that on my then fiancé who was anxious to adopt my son who was seven months old at that time. My mom said that she and my father would help with any costs. I was hesitant, but enough arm pulling made me cave in. I accepted with the condition that she wouldn't take over the wedding decisions. She agreed and said that she wasn't some crazy mother of the bride!

In keeping with my then fiancé's wishes, we were going to have a private ceremony, and a reception afterward for all our friends and family. The private ceremony was going to be in a park with the parents, siblings, and very best friends. I expressed these wishes early on to my mom, and the invitation was cleverly worded, "You are invited to a reception to celebrate the marriage . . ." My mom went on to say it was my wedding and my decision. So, lo *and behold, to my surprise she verbally invited a great-aunt, the darling grand-mother, some of her close friends, and whoever else! When my mom told me about who else was invited to the ceremony, I became pretty upset and told her to uninvite them. She told me she was doing no such thing, that if I wanted to be a b**** about it, I could call them myself to uninvite them. In tears, I ex-plained to her the circumstances of why my then fiancé and I wanted a private ceremony. If I remember correctly, she stormed out of the house in a fit, and I sat there crying trying to figure out how I was going to tell my then fiancé about this. She then informed me the next day that she that uninvited them, but she could have left the guilt part out of it!*

I wanted to do something fun at the reception, like passing around a jour-nal for people to write words of wisdom or whatever . . . Mom thought that was a stupid idea, so it was shot down. I wanted to make favors, and she tried with every ounce of her energy to shoot that down, but I made them anyway. I couldn't afford a DJ, so I was going to rent something at a rental place and get some wedding music to play for people to listen to at the reception. She informs me this is also tacky and wants me to get the band that her mother had at her sixtieth birthday party. I do not remember how this band sounded, other than it was small and country. My husband hates country. My mom informs me that it is tacky to not have dancing at a reception, so I grudgingly tell her to get this band. I should have said no!

Some moms are known for exerting their will on the wedding-planning process by labeling everything they dislike as "tacky." Etiquette is only convenient when it suits Mom's agenda but it can be discarded if it interferes with her desires.

While I would never counsel someone to be flagrantly disrespect-ful of her mother, there are times when it is best to sit back and ob-serve the behavior calmly as if you were a field scientist documenting

the courting rituals of the dodo bird. An attitude of scholarly be-
musement while you continue with your wedding plans will help you
to avoid evolving into the demon spawn child who has to screech to
declare her choices. Then resort to reference to a third party for etiquette cover. "That's okay, Mom, Miss Jeanne on etiquettehell.com
says not having a band is actually okay and not tacky. But thank you
for that suggestion. That was very kind of you to be thinking of creative solutions and ideas."

Rule 10: Extending Courtesies to the Extended Family

*My cousin Patty got engaged to her boyfriend and was set to marry him six
months later. She lives on the West Coast, with our other four cousins. My sister
and I live in the Northeast. None of the cousins are very close to Patty, but my
other four have grown up around her in the same state so they are a little closer to
her than my sister and I are. I accept her invitation and make reservations to fly
out. I am a poor college student but was excited to go anyway. I don't see this side
of my family enough and was looking forward to seeing everyone and having fun
at a wedding. I couldn't afford anything nice off her registry—the teaspoons alone
were $45—so I wrote a check for $100 as her gift.*

*One month before the wedding, Patty tells me that all the cousins will be in
charge of working different refreshment "stands" at her reception. Okay. I'm flying all the way out there to man a refreshment stand? She tells our male cousins
that they are in charge of being bouncers—throwing out guests who have drunk
too much, not serving too much alcohol, etc. Please note that one of my male
cousins is a Mennonite—he doesn't believe in any kind of violence or fighting.*

*I swallow all this, deciding it isn't worth making a fuss, and fly to the
wedding. I spent the week taking my cousin out, spending nearly $60 on her
at her stag. Two days before the wedding, I go to her house to ask her the way*

to the church. She says, "Oh, didn't I tell you? The church is so small that I'm only inviting close *friends and family.*"

So she's making me do all this work at the reception and I'm not even invited to the ceremony? I was flabbergasted. She gave me directions to the reception and told me I will be stirring punch and serving it. She also gave me a list of people not to serve. I asked her why I couldn't serve these people, and she said she'd seen them get drunk before and didn't want them to "ruin her wedding." She also informs me she'd really appreciate it if I cut my hair, as it was getting too "stringy" and "wasn't flattering." This is all two days before the wedding.

I arrive on time to the reception site. There are several other guests milling around, no other family, nobody I know. She has invited all the other family members to the ceremony except me. I know we didn't know each other that well and lived far away, but it was still so hurtful and tacky. Would one person more—a first cousin—have "ruined" the ceremony? I ran to the bathroom and started crying.

Well, to sum up the reception, I gave every guest punch, claiming I lost the list, and didn't hear two words from my cousin the entire time. I had spent over a thousand dollars to fly to a tiny town in Oregon, work at a punch stand, and not get invited to the ceremony. I never got a thank-you note, either. I chalk it up to a very hurtful and expensive learning experience. Brides, please don't do this to your families!

This falls under the category of "taking your family for granted" where it is presumed they exist for the sole purpose of being used as slave labor for your wedding. If you wouldn't invite these cousins to your wedding under even the best of situations, why would you even consider asking them to help with the wedding preparations? What chutzpah! The audacity of some brides is as breathtaking as getting sucker-punched when you least expect it. The truly obnoxious are also the truly obtuse and may ponder for years why certain family members avoid them like the plague.

Rule 11: It Could Be Worse . . . A Lot Worse

When you are tempted to think of your mother as the wedding-planning harpy, consider what kind of parents some people get stuck with.

> *As a criminal prosecutor, I was amused one day to see on my docket an assault case that was alleged to have taken place at a wedding reception. Living in a city where cultures and traditions often cause wedding guests to drink too much, this was not too surprising—until I saw that it was the mother of the bride who was accused of assaulting the maid of honor! At trial, we heard from the best man, the maid of honor, another bridesmaid, three wedding guests, and the father of the groom as prosecution witnesses.*
>
> *From the testimony we learned that the mother was not happy about the marriage, as the bride was forced into getting married because of her pregnancy. The groom was the father. It seems the couple had held their reception in the groom's backyard—complete with several kegs and a few picnic foods. After a few hours of drinking, the guests saw the "happy couple" leave for their honeymoon. The father of the groom decided that, as it was his son's house, he now was in charge. To show his "power," he apparently told everyone that it was time to go. The maid of honor and the best man (an engaged couple) along with the groom's friends and family immediately started folding up the metal chairs, throwing away plastic cups and plates, and generally cleaning up and shutting down the party.*
>
> *The mother of the bride and some of her friends and family seemed greatly*

insulted by the groom's father attempt to take charge of the reception, as "it was the bride's family who was supposed to be in control." The father of the groom testified that the mother had been drinking heavily that afternoon and was "popping pills." He further said that the mother of the bride began yelling at him for not showing her and her family proper respect and that she stated she would leave when she was good and ready. The father of the groom admitted that he called the mother a few choice names and told her to move her (rear end) or he would do it for her. A wedding guest claimed that some of the groom's family tried to get the mother to stand up and leave, but she instead lurched out of her chair and began cursing at everyone. According to this guest, the mother was approached by the best man (who looks like a bouncer), who told the mother in no uncertain (i.e., crude) terms that she had to go.

Testimony showed that the groom's side somehow got the mother to stumble over to the garage through which everyone had gained access to the backyard. From what the best man told the jury, the mother then began screaming how she was going to get even with the best man for this. Just then the maid of honor came out of the garage where she had been piling up chairs and ended up standing just behind the mother. The maid of honor stated that the mother turned, saw her, and swung her fist directly into the maid of honor's chest while screaming that she would get the maid of honor too. Statements conflicted as to how hard the blow was, but all the prosecution witnesses stated that it knocked the maid of honor over. The best man said that he grabbed the mother's wrist to stop her from hitting the maid of honor again, and that he was attacked right then by the bride's family who pulled the mother from his grasp and quickly pushed her through the garage and into a van parked in the driveway.

The defense testimony was that a brawl almost broke out at that point. The mother of the bride tried to act like a victim at trial and claimed she was under attack by the maid of honor. She claimed to have swung at the maid of honor as she "feared for her life." (This is the exact statement that a police offi-

...cer usually makes when justifying pulling his or her weapon on someone.) The mother claimed the maid of honor was "towering over her" while screaming and punching the mother. Her story began to fall apart when I asked that she stand next to the maid of honor and the jury could see that the mother was taller by several inches and was built much more substantially.

Frankly, by the end of the trial I was pretty disgusted with everyone involved for how they had acted, but the jury decided that the mother of the bride, in fact, had attacked the maid of honor and therefore handed down a guilty verdict for simple assault. After the trial I shook hands with the defense attorney (most attorneys understand that this is a job and not something we can take personally) and mentioned to him that I could not see the marriage lasting more than a few months. He chuckled and told me the bride already had filed for divorce. He told me later that they at least had not finalized the divorce until the child was a month old.

I think a lot of us would gladly put up with Mom's goofy handmade favors, her insistence on a shiny white wedding dress, and similarly innocuous demands if it meant not having a psycho mom with a criminal record.

Brideweena's Checklist

1. Have I remembered to suck in the foul, dank air of offense and count to a million before losing my temper?

2. Have I made a list of my priorities and what I am willing to negotiate away in order to compromise with family?

3. Have I communicated as effectively as I can to avoid misunderstand-ings?

4. Have I presumed upon family as owing me favors?

5. Have I read all of www.etiquettehell.com so I can blame Miss Jeanne for all of my positions on etiquette when my future in-laws throw a fit about the lack of a garter toss?

Dénouement

Brideweena and Curtis United in Marriage

Smallville Daily Tribune

Miss Brideweena and Mr. Curtis of Smallville were united in a double-ring ceremony August 24 at 2 P.M. at Holy Saints First Church of Smallville. The Reverend Syl Phasser officiated.

The bride is the daughter of Ethell and Stuart, of Smallville. She is a 1998 graduate of Ivy League University and is employed as a dancing instructor with Twinkle Toes Dance Academy.

The groom is the son of Mrs. Curtis Sr. and the late Curtis Sr.

He is a 1996 graduate of Academic State University and is employed with Tiny Words Publishing Company.

The church was decorated with bundles of white roses amidst live greenery sprinkled with fine fake snow by White Bunny Florists. The altar area was awash in the candlelight of three candelabras as well as two groups of evergreen trees covered in twinkle lights and more fine fake snow. Before the processional, guests enjoyed a dance processional by Brideweena's youngest dance students to the song "You're the Center of My Joy."

Brideweena then processed to "The Voice of Joy" by Wendy and Mary and was met halfway by her groom, Curtis, and they processed together to the altar. Her gown was a candlelight ivory Regency-era style with an empire waist, small capped sleeves, and a gold lace overlay skirt with a short train. She also wore a fingertip veil trimmed in white satin. The bride borrowed her mother's twenty-fifth-wedding-anniversary diamond ring to wear on her right hand. She carried a bouquet of gladioli, white roses, and fern. Curtis wore a charcoal gray morning suit with a paisley vest in shades of charcoal gray.

The matron of honor was Mrs. Muffin Louise, friend of the bride, of Youngsville. She wore a navy blue, two-piece dress with sweetheart neckline. Bridesmaids were Miss Tiffany, cousin of the bride, and Miss Angelique, a friend of the bride. The bridesmaids wore color-coordinating dresses of different styles and carried small fabric pouches filled with flowers.

Miss Honore, sister of the groom, was the groom's best "man." Mr. Derrick and Mr. Dexter, both friends of the groom, were groomsmen. The men wore charcoal gray morning suits while Miss Honore wore a dark gray evening gown.

Ushers were Mr. Byran, friend of the groom, and Miss Amelia, friend of the bride. Miss Courtney presided at the guest register. Misses Andrea and Phoebe were the program attendants.

A reception was hosted by the parents of the bride in the church's adjoining assembly room immediately after the ceremony. The room was decorated with long swaths of ice blue tulle hung in swags from the ceiling, large floor palms decorated with white twinkle lights, and handmade crystal snowflakes hung from the ceiling. Guests enjoyed an hors d'oeuvres reception consisting of cubed chicken with dipping sauces, vegetable crudités, fruit with chocolate dipping sauce, various homemade cookies, cheese and crackers, chocolates, nuts, punch, coffee, and hot cocoa. The groom's cake was a devil's food cake in the shape of a basketball in recognition of his favorite sport. A wedding cake of yellow cake with a strawberry custard filling was served. The bride's and groom's initials were on the cake in red mini-rosebuds. Aunts of the bride served punch and cake.

A rehearsal dinner was hosted by the mother of the groom at Stewart's Steakhouse in Templeton, Friday, August 23.

Brideweena's wedding day turned out to be a celebration of family, friends, and plenty of love. Her wedding was an exemplary instance of creatively incorporating elements that were uniquely representative of her and Curtis's tastes and interests but done so with graciousness toward the guests.

May your own wedding plans culminate in the perfect marriage of cooperation, graciousness, and gratitude that produces a joyous wedding day for everyone involved.

Dear Miss Jeanne,

Thank you so much for graciously serving us in so many ways. Undertaking the coordination of Brideweena and Curtis's wedding was massive, and we appreciate your putting up with our idiosyncrasies and making it all that we wished for. Many of our guests said how delicious the food was. We also really appreciated your creative ideas and expertise, about which we received numerous compliments from our family. So much of what we did was inspired by you. Your advice also prevented some disasters. Most of all, thank you for being such a dear friend.

Love, Ethell